WORDS ARE MADE UP!

(AND OTHER THOUGHTS THAT HURT TO THINK)

JAY NORRY

Words Are Made Up!

...and other thoughts that hurt to think

Copyright © 2018 by Jay Norry
Cover Design & Author Photo: Dawn Norry/Dear23

Publishers note:
All rights reserved. No part of this book may be reproduced in any form by any electronic or mechanical means including photocopying, recording, or information storage and retrieval without permission in writing from the author.

ISBN-13: 978-1-944916-73-2
ISBN-10: 1-94491673-3

Sudden Insight Publishing
Indie publishing for the Indie Author
www.suddeninsightpublishing.com

WORDS ARE MADE UP!

(AND OTHER THOUGHTS THAT HURT TO THINK)

CONTENTS

FOREWORD 7

THE DARK AGES WERE ACTUALLY DARK! 15

RESURRECTION USED TO BE COMMON! 21

SOME REHABILITATION ACTUALLY WORKS! 29

MEN ARE RAPED MORE THAN WOMEN IN AMERICA! 35

A SLAVE BY ANY OTHER NAME! 43

ABRAHAM LINCOLN WAS RACIST! 51

ECLIPSE BLINDNESS IS GREATLY EXAGGERATED! 57

THE DARK SIDE OF THE MOON ISN'T ACTUALLY DARK! .. 63

WE'RE RUNNING OUT OF PLACES TO LIVE! 69

MODERN DOCTORS DON'T TAKE THE HIPPOCRATIC OATH! .. 77

DOCTORS ARE PRESCRIBING ADDICTION! 83

EVERYONE'S DAY IS TWENTY-FOUR HOURS! 89

MINIMUM WAGE PREVENTS ENTRY INTO THE JOB MARKET! 97

EQUALITY CREATES INEQUALITY! 105

MAKING LIFE HARD MAKES LIFE EASIER! 113

THE WORLD IS ALWAYS ENDING! 119

VOTERS DON'T READ WHAT THEY VOTE ON! 127

AMERICA HAS MORE LAWS THAN ANY COUNTRY IN HISTORY! 133

WEATHER FORECASTERS GET PAID TO BE WRONG! 139

WORDS ARE MADE UP! 147

FOREWORD

This is the second book in this series, although you don't have to read the first to enjoy this one. Each chapter is centered around a particular topic in this book, just like it was in 'Earth is in Space! (and other thoughts that hurt to think)'. Aside from the fact that one chapter sometimes foreshadows what is to come in the next, and a few references are made to topics covered earlier, you could even read the chapters completely out of order and not feel lost at all.

Like any foreword, this is here to give you an idea of what's to come. The best way to do that in this instance is to let you know why this series of books was written, and how this idea came about in the first place. Then we'll get on to the disclaimers, since the current social and political climate can be an uncomfortable place for anyone looking to freely speak their mind on whatever pops into their head.

You know how sometimes it seems like you're having the same conversation over and over? The same topic comes up in multiple exchanges, over days or weeks or years; and sometimes it even finds its way into those first few thoughts you find yourself thinking in the morning when you wake up. One moment, you're feeling calm and clear and well rested; the next, you're wondering why they call it the dark side of the moon when it isn't actually dark.

Maybe this doesn't happen to you, but it certainly happens to me. Years pass, I meet new people, and we marvel over the same frighteningly fascinating kinds of things. The list grows as time goes on, since few of these issues ever get resolved for good; and after awhile I found myself with a fat file in my mind with no label on it.

The label part was easy enough to take care of. When I thought about writing this sort of thing, I pictured it in book format; but when I considered how I might best present it initially, I decided on a weekly blog. Each week I would cover some topic that I pulled from that file, and share it with the world for free. After enough of them had been posted publicly for awhile, I would take them down from that forum and compile them into books.

The blog came first, therefore; although the idea was first envisioned in book format. Soon I realized I had a much fatter file for this kind of thing than I had previously imagined, and I realized the blog would have to run for quite a bit longer than anticipated. Also, one book would not be enough. Right now, the plan is for eight books total; but I'm not betting anything of value on that. These are thoughts that hurt to think, after all; and there are plenty of those out there.

By the way...that's the title for the blog series, and the fat file in my head I keep referring to. 'Thoughts that hurt to think' seemed to encapsulate the idea pretty well, and it might still be running depending on when you're reading this. The first compilation is already out, and I mentioned it earlier; I'll mention it one more time, in case you want to hunt that title down as well.

'Earth is in Space! (and other thoughts that hurt to think)' was a very special book, for me. Although I have written a lot of books, and see each of them as uniquely rewarding, this was a whole new way to reach out to readers. We get to become friends, after a fashion; even if the conversation may seem one-sided. Just like if we lived near each other, or worked together, you get a glimpse of what I really think about and talk about with other people. And it's not one-sided, not really.

When a conversation isn't interesting to anyone involved, they tend to drift off and gravitate to other things. I have no problem with that, as an author; and I don't want to strive to keep someone's attention when we aren't into the same things. My goal and my purpose is to gather those precious people that are in my intellectual family about me and keep them close; by nature of being honest and sincere in that, I naturally push away the readers who don't see the sense in my brand of thinking.

So if you keep on reading, and enjoy yourself, we form a bond that really does go both ways; and if this kind of thing isn't for you, we drift apart and go on to other things. I have no issue with the people who aren't into what I write; I'm too busy being ridiculously excited about having readers who love my books. If that's you, read on with the knowledge that you have made me very happy by doing so.

Maybe you'll discover what I did, that hashing over these uncomfortable subjects makes them a little easier to live with. Maybe you'll realize you've had a lot of the same thoughts, and feel better knowing you're not the only one thinking them. And maybe you'll find yourself laughing at me, and wondering why I can't get past this kind of thing until I've thought it through and shared my musings with some friends. As long as you continue to enjoy reading, your reasons may remain your own.

I didn't set out to write an unusual kind of book, when this started; it all just happened naturally, and seemed to fit perfectly in the parameters I wanted it to. Finding my audience was always in the back of my mind, but I never really stopped to think whether I had read or enjoyed books like this before. This series is unique in ways I hadn't anticipated, and I couldn't be more happy to be adding another title to the set. You might put this kind of book on your coffee table, if you are looking to find the people in the room most worth talking to; or you might put it in a time capsule, to give folks a hundred years from now a common person's perspective on living in the world as it is today.

In the meantime, I hope the chapters in this book give you a good laugh. After all, one of the best weapons against unhappiness is a sense of humor. I try to keep things light, perhaps because the subject matter is so heavy; if I give you something to think about as well, then I have done the job I set out to do. I hope you love the book, and that you consider collecting all the titles.

Also, this series is best expressed in print format. I am grateful to you for reading the ebook, if that's what you're doing; but please consider picking up a print copy to have for your own. Ebooks don't sit on coffee tables or bookshelves like print books do, and they are a terrible thing to put in a time capsule. If you are accustomed to entertaining thoughts that hurt to think, you also know we could be plunged back into the dark ages at any moment by a dozen catastrophic possibilities. If that happens, you might be one of the few that survive; and if you survive, it would be nice to have something to read.

It kind of hurts to think about, doesn't it?

Well, get used to it!

As far as disclaimers go, I think we've just about covered that already. These subjects are things I've heard about, or read. I do my research on them, to be sure; but the whole thrust of this is to express these thoughts as I have heard them or had them. Getting too precise about where I first got this information would be misleading, since my views on most of this have changed with time. Nobody needs to have any of this stuff attributed to them, and most people wouldn't want to. It's the kind of conversation you have when you first meet someone that thinks about this kind of thing, not a scientific study on any of these topics.

Some of this could be wrong, even; the last thing I claim to be is correct about everything. When it comes down to it, though…even if only a little bit of this is true, it's amazing more people don't go crazy thinking about it all day. So let's talk about this stuff, let's have a good laugh over it; and then let's get on with living in a world that sometimes doesn't make a whole lot of sense.

Thanks for reading!

All the best,
Jay

#017: THE DARK AGES WERE ACTUALLY DARK!

There are times to be grateful for meteors, and there are times to wish they had just gone and chosen another planet to bash into. It's hard to even get historians to agree on when the dark ages actually were, and evidence points to future generations lumping us right in there with the past ones once our time is over. Thanks to those icy invaders from space, we can all agree on two things at least.

First, nobody wants to see a giant meteor crash into the planet anytime soon. We might be glad for the ones that came before, since they made it impossible for giant reptiles to thrive and very easy for large mammals to; but nobody wants to see the Earth's plant and animal life get decimated like it has so many times before.

Second, there have definitely been literally dark periods during our planet's history. Those falling chunks of rock and ice don't just cause massive tidal waves and dramatic climate shifts; they also trigger giant volcanic events, and kick up a bunch of dust. Can you imagine something big enough to shear off half the planet bashing into it, and leaving us with fifty percent of the land mass we had before? It doesn't matter whether you can imagine it or not; science tells us it happened, way back before the one remaining giant continent drifted across the planet to become seven. It's hard to figure, how much dust that kind of event might have kicked up; even without the resulting volcanic activity caused by chopping the tops off active volcanoes, the sky must have surely gone dark for days.

Right?

No, it was years. Decades, actually. Science also tells us that there were possibly periods of hundreds of years where there was no sun in the sky to see, if there was anyone there to see it. Now that, my friend, is pretty dark.

But it isn't what most folks call 'the

dark ages'. That phrase is reserved for people making discoveries in their chosen field, to be used on their predecessors. Even the guy who first came up with the term was later said to have lived in the dark ages himself, by folks in his own field. They stood on the shoulders of giants and cast dispersions on the quality of the view, as so many scientists do.

Oh, wait; that's kind of the entire premise for this book.

Anyhow, it becomes more and more apparent as time goes on that we can confidently interchange the terms 'the dark ages' and 'the past'. There's no reason to think we are at some pinnacle of human consciousness, unless we're poised to hand things over to the robots already.

Actually, maybe that is the answer. Why not program a robot to be the person we keep expecting our leaders to turn out to be, and put it in charge? We could even program it to keep promises, and keep its pants on the whole time it held office. You know, all those things we unreasonably expect from a person that couldn't possibly live up to them. Maybe then we would rise up out of the dark ages.

I'm not trying to kiss up to the robots, or anything; I have no reason to think any of them read my books. It just seems the direction we're headed in, together.

The robots will surely refer to our reign as 'the dark ages', once they get ahold of the system. It might be hard to refute their claim, since there really is quite a lot of evidence; it remains to be be seen if they will round us all up in camps and start using us as batteries or if they will give us world peace and free healthcare.

Have no doubt about it, however; the robots are coming.

The only thing that might stand a chance of taking them out is another giant meteor impact, and all that would do is bring the whole planet right back to the literal dark ages. It is estimated that these events happen on a pretty regular timetable, and that we're either slightly overdue or right on schedule for the next big one. So, now the question we have to ask ourselves is this: do we want robot overlords, or near annihilation? Do we want to stride into the future on synthetic legs, with the memory of us as creators being all that makes it into the robot mythos? Or do we want to live in caves again, and learn agriculture again, and build up society and governments and technology to the point where we face the exact same set of problems again?

I'm a little torn, from that perspective…

We humans seem to be bent on creating problems we can't solve, and mother nature has some pretty violent ways to address things like overpopulation and all the issues that come with it. People may have lived in numbers close to or exceeding our own, in the distant past; it's hard to tell, since all the evidence is obviously wiped out. We definitely know humans lived for long stretches of time with little hope and no sun after these timely tragedies have struck. And, also…we're due for the next one.

Dark, right?

Well, some of you know the reason I feel so comfortable delving into the darkness is because of my practice of dwelling regularly in the light. Some part of me can't let go of the thought that all this is unfolding exactly as it should, and that one thing will lead to another whether we fight it off or cheer it on. The serenity prayer offers even people with zero belief in anything practical advice, and a riddle to go along with it. I mean, who really knows exactly what is or isn't under their control? It may be that having the wisdom to tell the difference is the most important part of that equation, and the most difficult aspect of the riddle.

How are emotional beings with desires that enslave us as often as they set us free supposed to know our own power? It is in our individual nature to either seriously underestimate or grossly overestimate ourselves, or so it seems. So what is our destiny? Could it be to create something better than us, and then hand the world over to them? If the robots can come up with a way to put off the next mid-space collision that the universe has scheduled for us, maybe they should be the ones in charge.

No one wants to live in the dark, after all.

#025: RESURRECTION USED TO BE COMMON!

Back in the day, there were no heart rate monitors or machines that could detect brainwaves. You listened for a heartbeat, maybe put a mirror under someone's nose; but after they had failed those advanced medical tests, you were pretty confident it was time to put them in the ground.

Some cultures burn their dead, but the practice of burying the dead goes all the way back to the neanderthals. Again, there were no crematoriums back then; and the last thing you wanted the village fire to smell like was the roasting dead flesh of your fellow villager…so they started burying folks. We would call this a 'green burial' or a 'natural burial' in modern times, since there were no chemicals added to the corpse before they put it in the ground.

These aren't the only ways to get rid of dead bodies, of course. In the years since the first grave was dug by human hands, different cultures have come up with all kinds of ways to get rid of their dead. Although green burial is legal in all fifty states, not everyone can have a space burial or a ship burial; and you'll definitely have trouble arranging a sky burial in this country…but we're not here to talk about the different ways of burying dead bodies.

We're here to talk about resurrection.

The examples we generally think of when this word comes up are not people who clawed their way out of their tombs to walk the Earth looking worse than when they went in; but we'll also leave the great messengers out of this discussion, as well as any argument about the legitimacy of their individual resurrections. We're talking about normal people coming back to life, and walking among the living once more.

Even after advanced equipment started reading things like brainwaves, people still kept coming back to life after being declared dead. They still do, in fact. The reason it almost never happens is not because the tendency to resurrect has changed; it's because we generally relieve the body of all its fluids and replace them with chemicals before we put it in the ground now. All chances of coming back to life surely drain out of a body along with its blood; and nobody wants a messiah walking around stinking of formaldehyde, anyway.

Oh, yeah; we were going to leave them out of this.

Most people have heard of the different systems that were developed back in the day to make sure those that got buried alive did not remain entombed until they expired. The most popular version is a string that is tied to the corpse's finger on one end and a bell on the other. If the person moves, the bell rings; and they get dug up. Popular folklore tells of a system of this sort that was set up by a gravedigger who discovered fingernail marks on the inside of several coffins when they were dug up to be buried elsewhere in the cemetery.

Others say this is an urban myth, or an amalgamation of stories with similar elements that have been told all over the world. Either way, the thought of one person finding one set of fingernail marks on the inside of a coffin is enough to make me squirm…and that has definitely happened. Whether it was grave relocation, or an exhumation for an autopsy; or whether it was that village in Indonesia that digs up its dead annually to clean them up and give them fresh clothes, fingernail marks on the inside of coffin lids have been found too many times to mention.

I used to think the term 'dead ringer' came from the bell tied to the finger practice, but a lot of research into the meaning and the power of the ringer wised me up on that one. The comparison is not being made between someone you thought was dead and someone standing before you alive, after all. It's a term from horse racing, where a slow horse lowers expectations and is replaced by a faster horse that looks just like the slow one at crunch time. In this case, the word 'dead' is used to mean 'exact'; like being dead right or dead wrong, the reference has nothing to do with actual death.

'Ringer' is a harder one to explain, as it traces its roots entirely through the mysterious slang history of the English. Like many slang terms, the meaning is accepted without ever being very well explained; common use turned the word 'ringer' into another meaning for 'duplicate' somehow, and so a dead ringer is an exact copy.

Which is still wrong, if you think about it. If it's an exact copy, you don't get better performance out of one or the other; they're the same thing! It may be more accurate to call it a 'zombie ringer', since it isn't quite dead in the exact sense of the word.

Don't worry, all my zombie books are just about zombies; and all my ringer books are only about ringers. I understand as well as the slang-makers that 'dead ringer' caught on while 'zombie ringer' never even came up, and I can see why as well as they did.

It just doesn't have the same ring to it.

The point is…even with modern medical equipment, life and death both remain mysteries in many ways. In order to take that magical element out of it as best as we can, we cancel it out with science wherever possible. Rather than let resurrection continue to be common, like it used to be, we prevent the dead from coming back to life by draining their blood and replacing it with formaldehyde.

It's akin to offering a service like abortion without taking into account the fact that most unwanted babies used to just get left in the woods to be eaten by predators or scavengers. The average life span goes up wildly when those pregnancies aren't completed or counted, and people don't come back to life when you fill them full of chemicals.

Thank God for civilization, right?

And speaking of God…someone should let the almighty know not to send any more messengers. We won't give them the opportunity to come back to life, and prove that they came from wherever messiahs come from. We'll drain their blood, replace it with chemicals and put them in the ground…and that's where they'll stay. We've got a messiah-proof system here, and it's worked pretty flawlessly so far.

Of course, you can get around that. Most people think they have no choice other than having their dead relatives pumped full of chemicals when they die, but they actually do. Despite the serious price paid by family members and the environment, most funeral homes won't mention that embalming the body is just one of many options. Before you go paying thousands of dollars to have someone pollute the planet on your deceased relative's behalf, you might want to look into the pros and cons involving this process.

It will keep the dead from coming back to life, to be sure; but there are other ways to guarantee that. Simply draining the blood actually does the trick, with no need to fill the empty vessel with this stinky and environmentally harmful substance. Then the body can decompose in a natural way; and although we can argue all day about what God may or may not have intended, this method is definitely what nature intended.

Not the draining of the blood; that was totally people's idea. Nature built us all to turn into food for the next generation; even if it's a little macabre, we've got to have some means to keep going. Eventually all those messiahs found their way back to the land of the dead, according to the stories. I guess resurrection doesn't permanently solve the problem of death, after all.

It did, however, used to be a lot more common.

Bringing people back from the dead may be impossible; at the very least, it's a miracle. However, bringing people back to life is not beyond the realm of possibility.

No matter how dark a person's original circumstances, optimism would have us hoping anyone can be brought back from the brink of darkness. Even the most hardened criminal may be able to be transformed into a happy and productive member of society, according to studies on prisoners in other countries.

We'll talk about how the prison system is set up in America, and how differently some other countries are doing things, in the next chapter.

#037: SOME REHABILITATION ACTUALLY WORKS!

More than one social critic has pointed out that the justice system in America should maybe be called 'the revenge system' instead. Whether you agree with the way the country treats criminals or not, you have to be pretty short-sighted to argue with this assessment. Even if we didn't have other countries to compare ourselves to, few of us would call prisons in America compassionate institutions.

Social pressure is a strange thing. It makes for some very pretty diamonds, but it crushes a lot of perfectly good rocks along the way. We can't say we don't know what life would be like without civilization, since modern day life exists on Earth right there alongside what we would call primitive life. Yet somehow we don't understand what we give up when we leave that life behind completely.

No, I'm not suggesting a nomadic return to the plains or the caves.

Just hear me out.

In a small tribe, every member is expected to contribute. This practice leads to people that live active long lives, who give as much or more than they take in that time. We know they don't die of old age at thirty, even though that was a fun myth for some of us to believe for awhile; they just leave unwanted babies in the woods, which brings their average lifespan down dramatically. Instead they live as long or longer than modern day people; but those lives contain something different than the modern life often does.

Human biology is not set up for a child to have their food handed to them for the first eighteen years of their lives. All we have to do is compare the number of tribal kids with ADD to the number of kids in supposedly polite society who have it, and that becomes clear. When kids hunt and fish and forage as soon as they are physically able to, a strange thing happens.

Actually, it's not strange; it's completely natural.

These teenagers aren't angsty. Anxiety and depression are virtually non-existent, even in youngsters; and suicide is not really a thought for any of them. Also, crime is a giant rarity; rather than lock someone in a cage or kill them for transgressing, most tribes exile the offending member. Those are super rare occasions, though; most tribal people never think of hurting another. It's just not part of their programming.

So what does this have to do with rehabilitation?

Well, it turns out most criminals feel disconnected from society as a whole. Even worse, many people that turn to crime feel as though society itself is responsible for their less than ideal living situation. The last thing I'm going to do here is argue that they're wrong or right about that; the point here is that locking them up doesn't help as much as actual rehabilitation could.

And what's the best rehabilitation?

You guessed it! These folks need to feel needed, like nearly all of us do. It's not a giant mystery of the universe, or anything; it's just biology! The prison system in Norway is leading the world in rehabilitating offenders, and a lot of people are starting to look to their example for ways to improve their own systems. What they have found is that they've been doing pretty much everything wrong.

We focus on punishment in the United States, and put that priority first. Rehabilitation automatically comes in last when you do this, though; the way you treat someone you think should be punished is a lot different than the way you treat someone you feel should be rehabilitated. It's no secret how prison guards treat their charges in America; but few of us wonder if the prisoners act the way they do because of that treatment.

One view says these are not people deserving of rights, the other asserts that everyone makes mistakes. It doesn't take a social scientist to figure out that people act like people when you see them as people, and behave like animals when that's how you treat them. And we don't need a thought experiment to see how it works…we have a country boldly going where none have considered going before, and we can see how logically this plays out in real life.

The thing is, this doesn't just affect the people who end up in the system. Everyone in any given country is at least somewhat aware of how many laws they have to follow, how likely they are to be punished for not doing so, and how they will be treated if they are caught. We end up right back at the argument that most of the people who turn to crime feel marginalized by their country in some way.

Some people think if you make prison sentences less harsh, it will encourage criminals to break the law more often. It even sounds like it makes sense, from a certain perspective. The problem is, it also makes sense from a certain perspective to steal from a rich person just because you're poor. These are both emotional assessments, and it turns out they're both wrong.

When a nation's people are not afraid of their government, crime rates drop drastically. The few countries where the people actually feel as though the politicians care about their welfare have so little crime compared to the rest of the world that it makes us all look a little primitive. In those places where a close-knit community is the center of everyone's life, very few people feel disenfranchised or marginalized. And how likely is a person going to commit a crime when they feel like they are living a life of meaning and purpose?

Depends on what your country calls a crime, I guess.

This is where social pressure becomes a positive thing, instead of an insufferable weight that feels like it's suffocating some people from day one. When our lives become pleasantly intertwined, they can begin to have the purpose and meaning we are biologically engineered to have. When we are treated like something less than the people making and enforcing the rules, an explosive social pressure is created instead.

But that's not all the prison system in America has got going on. In fact, we're barely scratching the surface here. Any discussion on imprisonment in this country has got to acknowledge the common joke bandied about whenever anyone faces jail or prison time.

Actually, not everyone; just men, in fact.

#038: MEN ARE RAPED MORE THAN WOMEN IN AMERICA!

We'll start out by stating the obvious here, and acknowledge that almost every rape in America is committed by a man. Although women have their own unique ways to ruin another person's life, most of them are perfectly legal. Even falsely accusing a man of rape comes with little or no consequence, when you're a woman; but I'm a guy, so I'm not allowed to talk about that.

I have my long list here, of things a white guy can't discuss; and that's right there at the top.

Like most women, most men are not out there looking to hurt or dominate or marginalize anyone. A few bad eggs make the world an uglier place for all of us, though; and it would be nice to solve this problem in the situations where it is being engineered to happen.

In prisons, for example.

We talked about how the prison system in America is more about vengeance than justice in the last chapter. No example is more telling than the story of the rapist. This only works if we go with the classic example, since we don't want to veer off into any of that subject matter I can't talk about. We won't use the example of the guy and girl who have a few drinks together and enjoy each other's carnal company, although that's rape now according to some people. We also won't talk about the man or woman who willingly submits to sex when they don't feel like it, and regrets the decision later. Or the man or woman who voluntarily returns repeatedly to the arms of the person they claim keeps raping them.

This story needs a clear antagonist and protagonist, and those scenarios seldom provide either.

The classic example a lot of us think of is the guy who overcomes a woman in a dark alley. She fights him off, but he subdues her and has his way with her. Her immediate trip to a police station enables investigators to gather all the evidence they need to find the guy and put him behind bars. And we all know what happens to rapists in prison.

Lots of men get raped in prison, but word on the street has it that rapists and child molesters get it the worst. Which is to say the punishment for raping someone is to get raped repeatedly yourself. As the years of a prison sentence stretch out, it's highly likely that a rapist will be raped way more times than they did it themselves.

For many people, that's fine with them. In a penal system based on vengeance, an eye for an eye just doesn't seem like enough; Old Testament justice is weak and lame compared to the punishment we mete out to prisoners in this country, and very few people raise a stink about it. In fact, it's probably fair to say that many family members of murder and rape victims would pay to watch their bully get bullied on a live feed. The best way to activate the callous and cruel side of anyone is to hurt them or someone they love.

Which is where this argument falls apart first.

A lot of people go to prison for non-violent offenses. In fact, a lot of people go to prison in America for doing things that many civilized countries don't consider criminal at all. They get locked up with hardened criminals, and often come out that way themselves. After years of fighting off rape and bullying, very few people would be the same. The main difference between someone who sold a dime bag to someone who should have been able to acquire it legally and someone who raped or murdered is the time they spend in there. Otherwise, their realities are essentially the same for that time.

Except one is a hardened criminal, and the other is just an entrepreneur that pushed the wrong product. Guess who is raping whom, in this scenario. These two people never would have met on the outside, and they certainly would have never had a sexual relationship. Both men are changed forever by these circumstances, and it's unlikely for the better. The natural reaction for these men is to desire justice, especially since justice is supposedly what put them both in this situation. Unfortunately, justice looks like revenge to them; just like it does to the rest of us. Someone will have to get hurt even worse than they did for them to feel better about their own situation.

It's not hard to find examples of women who feel they were blamed to some degree for being raped. Whether it's the clothes they were wearing or the street they decided to walk down, women have been criticized for the choices they made leading up to the incident. That's wrong, and most of us know it; a woman should be able to walk up and down dark alleys all night in little more than their underwear and not get raped.

But what about the guys?

Have you ever heard anyone say that you shouldn't do the crime if you're not ready to do the time? In a world where most parents would steal food if their children needed it and they couldn't provide it otherwise, we have to realize that right and wrong are relative to each person's situation. And in a country that has more laws on its books than any country in human history, we have to also realize that at least some of those laws are just there to pack the prisons. Are we really okay with locking so many of our citizens in a metaphorical dark alley wearing nothing but their underwear?

Does their being men make this more acceptable, or less wrong?

The woman who walks up a dark alley in little more than her underwear and gets raped is not at fault. She may, however, make the choice to not walk up those dark alleys in the future. The prisoner doesn't have that choice; he is likely to get raped repeatedly so long as he is being held captive, no matter how cautious he is. But we're okay with that.

He made his choices, after all.

But this is still only scratching the surface of what our prison system is all about in America. Rehabilitation through repeated rape may sound like an awful idea, and it is; but it doesn't start to sound like a completely nefarious plan until you dig a little deeper. We have to look back at the history of the country's penal system to get the long view on it, and wonder what purpose the government might have for privatizing prisons. We also have to wonder why certain ethnicities dominate the inside in numbers while being minorities on the outside.

When we put these things together, we see that an awful lot of black men in American prisons are being put to work and earning pennies on the dollar for their efforts. Some states can actually demand labor from prisoners without any compensation at all, and states with rules against forcing death row inmates to work are always fighting to change those laws. They want to put all the prisoners to work, and pay them nothing or next to it.

So, what's the problem? Inmates have always crushed rock, or stamped license plates; what's so different now?

The difference is that since prisons were privatized, inmates haven't been crushing rock or stamping license plates. They have been packaging and manufacturing products for sale, and those products are being made for major corporations. And remember, they're making pennies on the dollar; or no money at all. In fact, most slaves used to earn a better wage in this country. Very few slave owners didn't give their slaves some compensation for their efforts, and most of them were allowed to raise a family and move about as they pleased during non-work hours.

Prisoners may not deserve freedom, or opportunity to hurt or steal from someone again. Maybe they don't even deserve rehabilitation, since that's clearly the popular opinion in our country. But do they deserve to get raped repeatedly? Do they deserve to be put to work for nothing or next to it? Are we really all agreed that these people don't deserve to be treated like people?

We'll talk about how likely it is for a young black man to be caught up in this system, and find himself working for free, in the following chapter. If you have time to read that one and the one after it, that would kind of be perfect. They go together in their own way, like the last chapter and this one; then we'll get on to discussing a certain brand of darkness in a particularly light-hearted fashion.

#039: A SLAVE BY ANY OTHER NAME...

A lot of people think slavery doesn't exist in the United States any more, and some even think slavery has been eliminated worldwide. Although most folks are aware that a number of slaves were brought to America from other countries back in the day, they don't all seem to know that the circumstances of many people today strongly resemble the conditions slaves existed in yesterday.

They also often don't know the first slave was owned by a black man, but that's another subject altogether; you'll have to keep collecting these books if you want to read that one.

If anyone can claim the title of 'African-American', it's most of the people that were enslaved in the beginning of the United States' relatively short and brutal history. They came straight from Africa, unlike the rest of us. I mean…we can all trace our roots back to Africa, but very few people in America today came here after being born there.

Many of the slaves whose backs our country was built on were of white European descent, and even more of them were from Asia; but most of them were black, and straight from Africa. They were not allowed to vote or own property, and most folks know that; what a lot of people don't know is that most of them also received money for their work. It wasn't much, usually; and it was generally left to the slave owner to treat their slaves well in such respects… but you might be surprised at how many slaves in early America were able to buy their freedom with the money they had been paid by the person they were buying that freedom from.

Things are much different now.

In modern day America, there are more black men in prison than there were slaves back then. It sounds like a strange comparison to make, but stay with me; the similarities will be quite clear if you keep reading.

Very few of the people locked in prison in America are violent offenders. Nearly everyone agrees it's wrong to physically attack another person, or steal from them, or rape them; and most of us feel more safe knowing people with such tendencies get removed from society. Some of us would rather see them rehabilitated than punished, since we know society is quite possibly the one that owes the debt; but we already talked about that.

This is another subject altogether.

What surprised me, when I found out, is that the vast majority of people in prison are not violent offenders. They aren't thieves, either. In fact, most of the people in prison are there for drug offenses. In case you don't know, drug use is as popular among white people as it is black people. It's just way more common for black people to get thrown in prison for these practices.

That's just ridiculous, right?

I said something of the sort, the first time I heard about this situation. I thought it was surely exaggerated, how much racial profiling determines who gets put in prisons in America. Then I was working with a guy, and he told me about his morning.

On his way to work, this friendly fellow had been pulled over. It was first thing in the morning, but for some reason the officer that did the pulling over asked my co-worker if he had been drinking. He said no, and repeated the answer as he was asked if he had any illegal drugs or weapons in the car. The officer didn't believe him, apparently; because he asked if he could search the vehicle.

At this point in the story, I was flabbergasted. I interrupted him, and pointed out how ridiculous the situation was.

"Did you say no?" I asked. "Did you tell him he needed both probable cause and a search warrant to go through your personal belongings, and that he clearly had neither?"

My co-worker laughed at me, in the most friendly fashion.

He didn't think this was ridiculous, or unusual; he told me it happened to him at least a couple times a month, and that he had heard stories about black men who said 'no' when a police officer asked to search their vehicle. He knew he had to do what he always did, and he let the guy search his car. It took awhile, since there were a lot of tools in the trunk; but after a thorough search, the officer let him get on with his day.

I couldn't believe it. What I found even harder to believe was the fact that my co-worker wasn't angry about it at all. He thought it was totally normal, and had long since accepted that he should be expected to be treated like a suspect every time he encountered a police officer.

My friend had never been arrested, and was actually a veteran. For those of you wondering, wonder no more. Also, he wasn't doing anything to warrant being pulled over. None of his lights were burnt out, and he wasn't weaving in his lane. He was just driving, and being black.

This was in California, not some part of the country that is typically associated with behavior of this sort. My co-worker was from the deep south, and he said it was way better here than it was there.

Somehow, that didn't make me any less angry.

It wasn't until later that I realized what

this meant. I found out that prisons had become privatized institutions just prior to the big rush to fill them to overflow, and these privately owned businesses were being paid for every prisoner they could pack in there. Then I found out prisoners were being forced to work at a fraction of a fraction of minimum wage, and the pieces came together at last.

Prisoners do more work for less money than slaves did back in the day. They don't get to vote, even after they are released from servitude; and getting a decent job with a criminal record is difficult to impossible. Most of them end up right back in the very institution that programmed them to believe they don't belong in polite society anymore.

It might be easy for some to ignore this situation, or pretend it doesn't exist. There might even be folks laughing at me right now for referring to our country's prisoners as 'people', when they are clearly seen as something less by the powers that be. I wonder if they considered it deeply when the first black president acknowledged the problem, and admitted that he avoided imprisonment 'only by the grace of God'.

Or maybe they listened to what he said about the wage gap and whistle-blowers and closing down Guantanamo, and realized that this guy was as full of it as all the others that came before him. When he signed a law enabling the government to imprison American citizens indefinitely without trial or due process, it certainly brought his credibility into question for a lot of people. That means we're now all one step from being slaves, free labor for private institutions that get paid for imprisoning us by the government.

This situation might not seem serious until you look at what kind of work these prisoners are doing. Most of us might think of rock crushing or license plate stamping when we think of incarcerated people working, but that changed right along with the privatization of these facilities. Now prisoners create products for corporations, and prisons have another stream of income to buffer their business.

I won't call out any companies, but I will suggest you search it.

Every time I hear someone complain about products being made in other countries by workers being paid next to nothing to be sold in ours at a huge profit, I can't help but think of this situation. The same thing is happening right here in our own prison system, and many states don't require that these slaves be paid any wage at all.

Oops…did I say slaves?

Sorry, I meant prisoners.

Now that prisons are privatized, I guess private citizens can own slaves after all. So, really…we're right back where we started. Except now there are more black men in servitude to the prisons than there ever were to private citizens in this country's history. When you put it that way, it seems as though Abraham Lincoln actually did more harm than good. Since he clearly stated that his aim was not to abolish slavery but to form a federal government, all kinds of things then fall on his shoulders.

Whether we can hold Lincoln responsible for the state of prisons today or not is up for debate, I suppose. But when you look at how he thought African Americans should be treated after they were freed from slavery, there's one thing you can't deny.

#040: ABRAHAM LINCOLN WAS RACIST!

It doesn't take much digging to find out what motivated Abraham Lincoln to go to such great lengths to fight slavery. He said it himself, according to history books; the issue was not as important as the cause. He would have been willing to hitch his wagon to any socially charged issue that came along.

And slavery came along.

Lincoln wanted to be able to tell everyone what they could and couldn't do, and pass that ability on to future administrations. He was not pleased with the restrictions placed on his power by states being allowed to run themselves. In many ways, this particular president single-handedly did more harm than any other president before or since.

He formed the federal government.

History makes no bones about Lincoln being fine with slavery in some instances, or vocally opposing abolitionist opinions of his time. In his quest to create an empire, Lincoln was happy to keep slavery legal in some states while he made it illegal in others. The cold heart beating in this man's chest was after political power, not equal rights.

As a matter of fact, Lincoln thought most of the freed slaves should be returned to Africa. Even when he finally allowed that they could live in America, he stated they should have a fraction of the rights white men had.

Lincoln didn't think freed slaves should be allowed to vote, or own property. In fact, he thought those rights should only be allowed to white men.

Thinking one ethnicity is better than the other is actually the definition of racism. It's hard to see how people can look back on this leader's attitudes and call him anything but racist. As far as forming a federal government, he did succeed at that.

All of the hard work the founding fathers put into building this country changed course completely in one fell swoop, and nearly all the things they were trying to avoid by giving states power to rule themselves have since come to pass.

Thanks, Honest Abe.

We couldn't have done it without you.

I've always wondered why Lincoln's spouse usually doesn't bear his name in the history books. Most of us know Mary Todd was Abraham Lincoln's wife throughout his entire presidency, but few people refer to her as 'Mary Lincoln'. Back then it was rare for a woman to keep her maiden name, or even hyphenate; but what about Mary Todd?

Rumor has it this woman may have saved the country from Lincoln's arrogant blundering on a regular basis. Apparently the esteemed president would write scathing letters to people when he was upset. The letters insulted the recipients, berating them for lacking character or fortitude or ability or all three. He would give them to her, and tell her to send them out with the mail.

Mary Todd would hide these letters, until 'Honest Abe' cooled off and came back asking if she had sent them. She would say no, and they would burn the letters together and maybe have a good laugh over what a psycho he was. One can't help but wonder what else she put up with.

It turns out President Lincoln had a bit of a temper.

We just don't get to know how bad it really was, since Mary Todd managed to soften the blow when he exploded. What else did she keep to herself, to make him look better?

Did she ever dare to mention that maybe the president should consider giving women equal rights, even if it was only white women?

I mean, clearly he was racist; but he must have been sexist as well. Otherwise Lincoln would have fought for the rights of women, instead of focusing on forming a federal government.

Maybe that's why Mary Todd went down in history books with her own name. She may have realized her husband was both racist and sexist, and perhaps she didn't want to be associated with that any more than she had to.

It would have actually been pretty clever of Mary Todd, to insist that she be referred to by her maiden name.

People like me will forever wonder if she saw the way her husband conducted himself and decided to make a clear statement that she was not part of that.

Imagine if all those hateful missives had found their intended recipients. What if Mary Todd had not been there to intervene, and make her husband look like a decent and considered man?

Even back then, the guy was super famous. You can bet the people who never got those letters would have kept them and sold them at some point, and plenty of collectors would still have the originals today.

We could read copies of those childish rants on the internet, in his own hand. Maybe then we wouldn't put him on such a pedestal.

The image I had of Abraham Lincoln was much different before I found all this out. Rather than hate on the guy too much for going to such great lengths to change the entire purpose of America, I should admire him for marrying such a good woman.

To this day, many people think Abraham Lincoln was a great man; surely those opinions would be different if Mary Todd had not carefully cultivated this image for her husband.

To sum up…

Slavery was not something Abraham Lincoln ever wanted to get rid of. He used a popular issue of his time to get what he wanted, which was a federal government. Even after the slaves were freed, he didn't think they should have equal rights; rather than offer them the ability to vote and own property, Lincoln thought they should be sent back to Africa. The Thirteenth Amendment, which most people think finally did make slavery illegal, didn't even do that. Those key words at the end tell a different truth.

"Except prisoners."

So don't let anyone tell you slavery is illegal in America; in fact, business is booming more than ever! Also, don't fool yourself into thinking Abraham Lincoln was all about equal rights. He was racist, and sexist; otherwise he would have conducted himself a lot differently while in office.

Now it's time to lighten things up a bit.

Let's talk about blindness, eclipses, and darkness.

ECLIPSE BLINDNESS IS GREATLY EXAGGERATED!

Last year, a lot of people got excited about the eclipse; for a few days, it seemed like it was all anyone talked about. I remember being curious about the difference between a solar and lunar eclipse when I was a kid, and hitting the books to find my answers; but that was as far as my curiosity went back then. It wasn't until this most recent event that I got to wondering about something else, and luckily all I needed was a good search engine to find answers this time.

You've probably heard it your whole life, like I have; but we probably both heard it a lot more in those weeks before the last eclipse. No one should look at the sun during a solar eclipse, because…

Well, you know why.

It will blind you!

Right?

Uh, actually…

I started wondering if that was one of those things they told you, like all those other things they tell you, when you are young and prone to believe what you are told. In this case, even I believed looking at the sun during an eclipse would blind you. Almost my whole life. In fact, right up until not all that long ago.

That's why this chapter doesn't have a number in front of the title, like the others do. I thought of it at the last minute, and posted the blog by that name as a bonus post on the day of the eclipse. Several posts were already scheduled, and I had foreshadowed the next regularly scheduled post; so this one didn't get a number. And…this seemed like the perfect place for it, in the book. There's nothing like debunking an urban myth, to lighten things up; and we definitely need to lighten things up, after the last few chapters.

So, let's do that.

The first thing I found myself wondering about, when I wondered about this, was how many people there were in the world that were blind because of looking up at the wrong time. I have great faith in people, and even greater faith in their ability to do monstrously stupid shit. Somebody somewhere had to hear the old saying about being blinded by an eclipse and shrug it off, right? With billions of people on the planet, the number of people without vision because of this must be at least in the hundreds, right?

Wrong.

Want to know how many people have been completely blinded by an eclipse? Well, there aren't any. You will find people with spots in their vision from staring at an eclipse for several minutes, and some of them even seek media attention in the days before and after these rare events; but you won't find anyone that has been blinded by glancing up during an eclipse. That's because it doesn't happen.

None of this is to say you should ever stare at the sun. That's bad for your eyes almost any time, and it's especially dangerous right before and right after a total solar eclipse. Young people particularly should always avoid looking at the sun, since their eyes are still developing. Although most people that experience diminished vision regain what was lost, some of that damage can be permanent. You won't go blind, or anything; but you might see spots the rest of your life.

Isaac Newton was blinded by staring at the sun through a telescope for an extended period, and his sight returned after three days. Most people who suffer any loss of sight from similar activities also regain what they lose. The ones that don't aren't blind, though; they just see afterimages every time they look at something. That may have been a scary three days for Newton, but it didn't stop him from continuing to study the sun. You can bet he caught a glimpse of an eclipse if he got the chance, and that didn't render him permanently sightless either.

Or anyone else, for that matter.

Some scientists that study the subject to this day think this is a terrible myth that has prevented people from seeing one of the most beautiful sights the naked eye can behold. During a total eclipse, there are often several minutes when staring directly at the sun is no more harmful than gazing at the full moon; which is to say, it's perfectly safe to do so. Although the people who study this stuff know better, it's hard to supplant a belief that is held by most modern people. So they look at this rare event while the rest of us look away, and they shake their heads at how our ignorance keeps us from beauty more often than it protects us.

I mean, maybe. As far as I know, maybe they don't think of how we think at all. They've got some pretty wondrous stuff to fill their heads with, those scientist types. What do they care what parents tell their children to keep them in the dark?

Or at least, from looking up during an eclipse.

If we want to change this common misconception, we end up with a similar uphill battle that we fight in trying to prove that the Robin Hood saying is wrong. There's this catchy little phrase most of us accept as fact, and we can't sum up the actual truth of the matter in just a few short words. Since we know kids can't stand to listen to adults drone on for more than one sentence or so, we make sure some of those sentences will stick with them.

Even if they're lies, and adults grow up to believe them too.

The truth is, you should only look directly at the sun during a solar eclipse. Glancing up from time to time to catch a glimpse of it won't mess up your eyes, even if you are glancing up right before or after a solar eclipse. What you need to avoid is gazing at the sun for long periods of time, whether it is in partial eclipse or not. However, the one time you can actually look directly at the sun for several minutes is while it is in total eclipse. Which is pretty much the opposite of what we are told by all those people who don't bother to find out for themselves before cautioning everyone against beholding beauty in this rare form.

We'll keep the discussion away from Earth just a little longer, so we can talk about another common phrase that simply isn't true. When opinions are regularly presented as facts and perception is often mistaken for reality, it's no wonder we can't even describe our own moon correctly without mucking it up somehow.

I mean, come on…

#043: THE DARK SIDE OF THE MOON ISN'T ACTUALLY DARK!

The first thing we should be clear on is that this discussion has nothing to do with Pink Floyd. I'm a big fan, but I'm not here to discuss whether or not one of their most popular albums was dark in tone or texture. In fact, we're not here to talk about Pink Floyd at all.

I don't know why you brought it up.

We're here to wonder why people make up phrases that other people know are wrong, only to have those other people repeat the phrase ad nauseam. In particular, we're here to talk about one especially annoying example.

Everyone knows the moon only ever shows us the one side. No matter how full or clear the moon is in the night sky, the part you can see always looks the same as it did the last time you saw it.

Most folks also know this is because the moon rotates at the same rate it revolves. We're going to get more into that another time; now we have all we need to do a little thought experiment.

If the moon is always facing one direction relative to the Earth, that has nothing to do with the way it is facing relative to the sun.

I mean, it does; but since Earth has day and night, so does the moon.

The only time the entire moon sees total darkness is when the Earth gets between it and the sun. This doesn't happen very often, and some folks make a big deal out of it when it does.

They make an even bigger deal out of it when the moon gets between the sun and the Earth; but we already talked about that, last chapter.

What we didn't talk about is what was happening on what we call 'the dark side of the moon' while it was eclipsing the sun in some parts of the world.

It was full daylight, there on 'the dark side of the moon'. It remained full daylight for a while, too...

Just like it does pretty much half of the time.

The part of the moon that is lit up when we see a mere sliver is only representing a tiny bit of the full light the moon is getting at the time. We just can't see it, because it's shining on parts of the moon we can't see.

I know, that's totally obvious.

Even if you never thought about it before, you only have to think about it for a few seconds to realize that pretty much every part of the moon enjoys daylight on a regular basis.

So why am I so annoyed with the whole thing?

Well, it's the saying.

You know the one…

'The dark side of the moon'.

I mean…it's wrong!

The dark side of the moon isn't actually dark, it just faces away from us! How arrogant are we, to call it dark simply because we can't see it? It's too much like that eternally bothersome question, if a tree falls in a forest and no one is there to hear it…

Does it make a noise?

Yes, you ignorant jackass!

There's a whole forest there, birds and bear and deer and elk…definitely coyotes.

Certainly rats and bugs.

If there's no forest, there's no tree; you can't separate it from its environment, or say the non-human denizens of the forest don't exist. They almost all have ears, or some way to sense sound; and a forest doesn't need people to exist or to engage its many hearing mechanisms. Supposing it does is like supposing everyone you interact with disappears between those interactions.

Or that the part of the moon you can't see is always dark.

Even though most of us leave such childish notions behind with childhood, we tend to carry a lot of these common sayings into adulthood.

If pressed, I have to admit that I've never called it 'the other side of the moon' or 'the side of the moon always facing away from us'. I've always called it 'the dark side of the moon' like pretty much everyone else, full well knowing the part of the moon I'm talking about gets plenty of sun.

Because then you know what I mean, instead of wondering if I'm deliberately trying to be a pain in the ass or if it's just in my nature.

Maybe I'll start saying 'the other side of the moon'.

(After all, it kind of is in my nature.)

Don't get me wrong in any of this; I love the moon. It's pretty, and it provides a variety of functions.

Besides being the object of this and other ridiculously untrue sayings, the moon makes life on Earth the way it is in many ways.

It gives us the tides, and the ability to experience day and night all in one place instead of inhabiting a planet that exists in perpetual darkness on one side and constant daylight on the other.

Also, we might have to live there one day. Since the moon is about the same distance from the sun as Earth, relative to other planets, it may be our first stop on the way to colonizing the cosmos.

Perhaps we'll look at living on the moon as an experiment, since supplies can be sent from Earth without waiting light years for them to arrive. When you take into account how many people there are on the planet, and how many ways we have come up with to tax it with our presence, you end up with a long list of thoughts that hurt to think.

It's no wonder we have a chapter dedicated to discussing that very problem coming up next. I hope you have time to read one more; but if you don't, no worries.

The rest of the book will be waiting for you when you get back to it.

Oh, who am I kidding?

What I *really* want is for you to go ahead and read one more.

#045: WE'RE RUNNING OUT OF PLACES TO LIVE!

Ever since humans discovered atomic bombs and nuclear energy, we have really left nature in the dust so far as horrific longterm planetary consequences go. The list of places where people can't visit without being exposed to harmful radiation keeps getting longer, due to more of that pesky inescapable logic. We are still building more bombs and nuclear energy facilities, without bothering to figure out a way to clean up the previous sites. While harmful radiation keeps leaking out of old barrels buried near valuable water supplies, we continue to draw up plans for new power plants that produce this volatile and dangerous energy. Even if the plans are perfect, scientists have to admit human error has caused more of the nuclear power problems than bad designs have.

They estimate the new plants we are building will cause four times the number of unlivable areas by the middle of this century than we have now. That's not counting the problems that arise from things like tsunamis and earthquakes, or the deadly combination of one happening right after the other.

But even if we err on the side of caution, and calculate in the most generous way possible, this situation still mathematically gets out of hand pretty quickly. Let's say there are five sites in the world that have been made uninhabitable by nuclear accidents or explosions or waste dumping. Let's also say we have been at it for a hundred years, and that estimates say we will continue at this pace for the next hundred years.

These are all wrong premises: there are more than five places made uninhabitable by nuclear radiation, we haven't been toying with this stuff for quite a hundred years, and estimates predict we will quadruple this number in the next fifty years. We're just being super generous in our calculations, to make the point that even the most optimistic mind will have to admit there is a problem here at some point.

If we continue at the rate of making five places on Earth uninhabitable every hundred years, it might be a while before the entire planet is unlivable. But while the number goes up by one every twenty years or so, it doesn't start to go down for any reason until a lot more time has passed. Nuclear radiation doesn't go away quickly, and tens of thousands of years may have to go by before the places we are making unlivable today are able to support life once more. Even though one new zone every twenty years or so doesn't sound like much, we have to remember that the number of places we have to live on this planet is far from infinite. In ten thousand years, even at the rate we are going in this generous calculation, there will be at least five hundred radiation hotbeds on Earth.

This doesn't take into account the number of barrels that have been dropped into oceans and lakes, or buried underground. Some have been put there legally, others not so much; but nature will erode both the legal barrels and the illegal ones at the same rate. When they start leaking, since radiation lasts way longer than metal barrels, new spots will start popping up all over the place where human life will have to be evacuated. And it can't return for tens of thousands of years.

That's just the best estimate we have, by the way. Since humans have only been working with nuclear radiation for eighty years or so, it's hard to accurately project that far into the future. The first estimations of how much radiation a human body could withstand were cut in half not long after the number was established, and then were cut in half again as longterm studies became more longterm with time. The honest truth of the matter is that we don't know what kind of results the existing situation will have in the next hundred or two hundred years, even if we do nothing to add to it.

If we do add to it, simple math shows us that the more we do so the less places we have to live. With human population still rising at an alarming rate, despite theories that the rise may slow down one of these days, we need more places to live; not less.

None of this takes into account the

number of places we can't live because of asbestos mining or oil spills or harsh natural conditions. At this point it's hard to say that any part of the world is untouched by nuclear radiation, since it radiates. Our atmosphere is all one big interconnected system, as are our oceans. One bomb going off anywhere on the planet will have consequences around the world eventually, as will one leaky barrel in a single body of water. When those numbers get up into the mind-boggling reality of our situation, the concept of longterm consequences kind of takes on a whole new meaning.

The frightening reality is that humans treat nature the way a toddler might treat a loaded pistol. We push and pull at the moving parts, let our curiosity get the best of us, and end up facing consequences beyond our scope of understanding. And that's just on Earth. Our best bet to escape our own mistakes is to get into space as quickly as possible, but then a whole new set of unforeseeable possibilities arises. If we can do this kind of horrific stuff on our own planet, what effect will we have on the universe once we get out there? Will we keep trying things just to see what happens, and then keep doing them even when we see that what happens is terrifying and irreversible?

You know, like we've been doing here on Earth?

Maybe we should hope there are no aliens out there, instead of wondering why they haven't contacted us. If every planet were seen as an individual and sentenced accordingly, the only attention we might get from a technologically advanced race could very well be whatever it takes to stop us from going any further in the direction we are already headed. If they judge us like we judge each other, alien intervention may be the worst thing that could happen to us. Rather than shame us on Twitter, they may just blast us into oblivion.

You know, for the overall good of the universe.

We might get all upset about what other countries are doing, here in America; but this is one instance where we really can't point a finger in any direction without having three pointing back at us. The United States has detonated more nuclear weapons than anyone, both in peacetime and wartime. The effects of those explosions have touched several generations already, and we honestly can't say what the planet would be like without whatever radiation is lingering from those countless detonations.

Okay, they're not countless; but counting them is scarier than tossing a blanket term over them all, so I'm sticking with that.

We might know what close proximity exposure to nuclear radiation does, but we have no way to measure what happens to the rest of us or the planet as a result of these bombs going off all over the world. The only way we could do that would be with a carefully controlled experiment of incredible scope and magnitude. Maybe, with this experiment, we would discover that we really are affecting the climate in a real and measurable way.

Hell, who knows? If we're going to talk impossible experiments and improbable scenarios, we may as well entertain a political conspiracy theory of the rare kind. Maybe the world's governments, or the world government, saw a long time ago that another ice age was coming. Maybe they realized the best way to forestall global freezing was to detonate some really hot bombs and industrialize in ways that deliberately changed the planet's climate. In this scenario, at least the folks in charge look like heroes for the people instead of power hungry sociopaths.

Not that I believe that; but it is just as plausible as people drawing up new plans for nuclear power plants and building new bombs when we still haven't figured out how to completely control the last batch.

And that's totally happening.

#048: MODERN DOCTORS DON'T TAKE THE HIPPOCRATIC OATH!

When I found this out, I was a little appalled. I had been told in school that all doctors were bound by the Hippocratic Oath, and that's why they couldn't do things like prescribe laxatives as a practical joke or end someone's life no matter how much pain they were in. It turns out doctors stopped taking this oath a long time ago, and just a little investigation pretty quickly shows us why.

I mean, have you ever actually read the Hippocratic Oath? I can't read Greek, but I have to assume the translation is pretty accurate. It starts out with 'I swear by Apollo the Healer, by Asclepius, by Panacea, and by all the gods and goddesses…'

Uh-oh. Most of the western world is pretty into a god that is often referred to as jealous, and not a big fan of other gods. As much as our statues and paintings of the supposed big guy in the sky might resemble old depictions of Poseidon or Zeus, we dispensed with all those old beliefs a long time ago. Who is going to take a modern doctor's oath seriously if he makes it to Apollo? Certainly not me, and probably not the doctor either.

Let's skip ahead, see what else it says…

The next paragraph is all about sharing your business profits with your teacher, and teaching the art of medicine to his family at no cost to them should they also take this oath.

That means medical students don't pay for their education, but they have to give the person that taught them part of the money they make from practicing. This might not be such a bad idea, as far as 'pay it forward' philosophies go; in fact, it makes an elegant sort of sense. It's definitely better than putting young people in debt to the point where they are more beholden to the money they can make than they are to doing the right thing.

However, this section does have one glaring problem. It refers to the teacher as 'he', along with the members of 'his' family you are allowed to teach this stuff to. So, no women are allowed to be instructed in practicing medicine according to the Hippocratic Oath.

I mean, I knew the guy was a little old-fashioned…but sexist?

By the way…we're just getting started.

The following section starts off strong, and all physicians really should have no problem agreeing to 'use treatment to help the sick according to my ability and judgement, but never with a view to injury and wrong-doing'. Even if that gives incompetent or uninformed doctors the wiggle room to kill a lot of people without ever really breaking the vow, it does cut down on pure unadulterated evil in medicine if everyone sticks to it.

But then, it really goes off the rails.

In the same paragraph, the oath states that the doctor swearing it shall never administer a poison. Even when asked to do so. That was all well and good when we thought leeches could suck sickness out of you, or that demonic possession was responsible for many ailments; but now we know that the best way to kill some really bad stuff is to poison it, and that some people with certain conditions are too far gone to ever recover.

We have to poison the patient to get rid of cancer, and some progressive states allow for the same mercy all the others extend to the average pet when it comes to euthanasia. Most of the states that allow capitol punishment do it with poison, too; that might sound creepy to some of us, but it's not nearly as creepy as a good old-fashioned hanging or death by firing squad. Even people who don't think criminals should be put down would have to agree that having a qualified physician administer poison is a lot more humane than those other methods.

But not the Hippocratic Oath.

In fact, it goes right on to forbid that the doctor perform abortion. Ever. For any reason. I don't really get the part that says the doctor won't use the knife on sufferers from stone, but that might be because I'm still reeling from the fact that the Hippocratic Oath forbids abortion.

Maybe they really needed unwanted babies back then, even if it meant the mother literally had to die for it to be born; but we have no shortage of people these days. Also, women really ought to have a choice.

And, of course, equal opportunity to become a doctor.

Not so, according to the Hippocratic Oath.

The next part reiterates the whole 'I promise not to hurt anyone' clause, which is maybe the baby we should have kept when we threw out the bathwater. It goes on to talk about the importance of keeping secrets, and how doctors in the service of their patients shouldn't go around blabbing about what is going on medically with those patients. It says those secrets should be holy, but remember who we're making this oath to. What's so holy about a Greek god no one worships anymore?

Like most good oaths, this one ends with the promise of a good life for the person who follows it and horrible misfortune for those who don't. A lot of people who believe in the oath think it starts with a phrase that is familiar to anyone who is at all versed in Eastern religion.

'First, do no harm.'

Although Hippocrates goes back pretty far, he doesn't go as far back as this saying. He may have tossed it in there, or not; but he certainly didn't come up with it. Many people think this is the basic gist of the oath, and they're mostly right; but mostly leaves a lot to be desired, at least in this case. As clear as it may be that modern doctors need to learn to put ethics above economics, this oath is not the path to modern ethical behavior. We would need to come up with something new, and then hope the temptation to pay off those student loans is not more compelling than the desire to follow through on the better oath.

Even if we give credit where it is due, taking away all the blame that would ordinarily accompany such praise, Hippocrates would not survive a day as a doctor in the modern world. He would be laughed out of any hospital or clinic for his beliefs and practices, and few people would believe that the foundation for what we do now was laid by someone so ignorant of the most basic medical knowledge of today.

So, yeah; maybe it's good that modern doctors don't subscribe to his philosophy any more than they prescribe his methods. Of course, what they are prescribing is scary in its own way.

#051: DOCTORS ARE PRESCRIBING ADDICTION!

The first time I heard there was a pharmaceutical version of heroin, I was pretty sure the person telling me so was exaggerating at least a little. Heroin has always gotten such a bad rap, for being so addictive and notorious for turning the people who use it regularly into junkies; even if they have a medical version of it, they must use it super sparingly.

Right?

Maybe so, back in the days when I first heard about it. Back then folks likened morphine to heroin, and rightfully so. The two are slightly different when outside the human body, but they become the same thing once they get in there. The dosage has to be adjusted, since heroin is about three times stronger than morphine; but the effects are virtually indistinguishable after that.

Perhaps we should clear up one common misconception, before we go any further. Most heroin overdoses happen because the substance is illegal. Dealers often look to get the most bang from their bag, and tend to mix all kinds of stuff with heroin to make the bag bigger. Whether they use crushed vitamins or something else to fluff it up, the stuff they put in there that isn't heroin is referred to as 'cut'. The users in a given area get accustomed their dealer cutting their product, and they adjust their dosage accordingly.

Then a pure batch hits the streets, and they don't adjust to account for it. Users take as much of the pure stuff as they did the cut product, and that results in an overdose. If this was a controlled substance, it would radically reduce the number of overdoses. The inconsistent strengths people buy on the street is what causes most heroin overdoses, and that variable could be eliminated by making it legal. Although personal responsibility plays a part, as it does with any aspect of life, we still need to take into consideration how the deck is stacked against any group being told what they can and can't do by the government.

Even heroin users. They're people too, after all. Not only that, their numbers are increasing due to more availability of prescription drugs that can be likened to heroin. Regular people who never had a hankering to shoot up before are taking it up in alarming numbers, due to more circumstances created by the powers that be. It's not uncommon for a minor injury to warrant a prescription for these drugs, and many of those prescriptions last just long enough to cause physical addiction. When the prescription runs out, the addiction is still there; so these folks hit the streets, looking for heroin.

That is, if the pills don't kill them first. Anyone who knows anything about drug use knows they don't have the same effect the tenth time as they did the first time. An increased dosage is required to reach the desired effect, whether the desired effect is a nice buzz or pain relief or getting blasted out of your mind. Although tolerances increase as the effect decreases, there are other factors at play here as well. See, the medical field has their own kind of cut; and it makes it into nearly every pain reliever on the market.

We won't get into the dangers of acetaminophen here, or how it is really what's behind nearly all these deaths we keep seeing from pain relievers; we'll just proceed knowing this is a low grade pain medication with tons of ill effects, and that it is put in nearly every over- and under-the-counter pain relief drug. It is added despite these horrible long term effects, and despite the fact that it is not necessary when you have an opium derivative already in there. As mentioned previously, the pain killing effects are pretty low grade.

That's where all these medications come from, either a natural or synthetic version of opium. The synthetic version of an opiate is specifically referred to as an 'opioid', but the category includes both natural and synthetic expressions of these powerful pain relievers. Each is uniquely formulated to last longer or deliver faster results or compound its results over time, but they all pretty much do the same thing. They relieve pain, for acute or chronic sufferers. That's all well and good when the pain doesn't last long enough to get the patient hooked, but that means we have some real issues on our hands.

People who suffer from chronic pain need a better alternative, for one. Jumping from one version of opium to another doesn't stop them from getting addicted, and that addiction often leads to the streets and the heroin we were talking about earlier. When the effects wear off, or the prescription ends, these folks move on to the street stuff more often than you might think. It's hard to imagine the landscape of addiction from the outside, but they wouldn't have a word for it if it wasn't real. At this point the addict doesn't have a choice in the matter, and heroin use has become immensely more popular among the middle and upper class as a result.

Even acute suffering should only be addressed with such strong stuff in extreme cases. Gritting your teeth through a little physical pain might be the better choice than getting strung out on heroin, and that is where this path all too often leads. Most of us were freaked out to hear that this pain reliever or that pain reliever was ten or twenty or thirty times more potent than heroin, but the most recent among the usual suspects already has a pretty grim track record. You can talk all you want about Vicodin or Oxycontin or Dilaudid, but none of them come close to the drugs like Duragesic and Sublimaze.

Yes, those should all be capitalized.

They're brand names, after all.

They fall into different categories, the last being the scariest. Those drugs contain fentanyl. They are estimated to be fifty to one hundred times stronger than heroin, and they are highly addictive. The habit forms in about eight days in most people, which is pretty fast; but that's not the most alarming part of the role these drugs are playing in opiate addiction. The most common length of time doctors are prescribing these drugs for in America is twelve days. Although they know how long it takes to become habit-forming, doctors are actually writing most of these scrips to extend four days past that mark.

Either I'm really bad at math, or doctors are prescribing addiction.

#053: EVERYONE'S DAY IS TWENTY-FOUR HOURS!

Politics have never really interested me, since I never wanted to be a politician. It was pretty clear to me when I was a kid that I would have to spend all day every day updating my knowledge of the country and the world just to stay informed enough to do a job like that. Even then, the difference between information and opinion gets pretty blurred on nearly every issue; figuring out if what you learned was the truth or a lie or a cleverly crafted half-truth would also take all day every day, and that means no time to learn that information in the first place. Also, it turns out many politicians have to spend pretty much all day raising money; so that leaves no time for either practice.

After hammering doctors for the last couple chapters, I should address their time issue here as well. To cover student loans and malpractice insurance and the costs of running a practice on top of their regular bills, doctors have to see a ton of patients in a day. The average length of time a doctor spends with each patient is around seven minutes, since they have so many costs to cover and so much paperwork to keep up on. Many of them quickly fall behind on keeping their education updated in a field that is always rapidly changing, because there just aren't enough hours in a day.

You can say that isn't enough time to spend with a patient, but they are stuck between a rock and a hard place in the modern landscape of medicine. If your only choices were getting your seven minutes or not having a doctor at all, which would you choose? Just be glad there are people passionate about helping people; the money isn't really there like it used to be.

Also, there are only twenty-four hours in a day.

Rather than eliminate the careers I didn't want to do one at a time, I spent much of my childhood reading books and wondering what I would be when I grew up. I didn't realize at the time that the people you admire can often help you figure out what your heart longs for, but I did know the people I admired most were authors. When I learned many of my favorite authors were somehow writing more than one book a year, I was amazed. Even writing one book seemed like a huge and complicated task to me; it wasn't until I had written several books that I saw how focus and practice play a huge role in an author's productivity.

    I imagine trying to become a politician or a doctor would give me insights into those fields that would turn any criticisms I may have into compassion; but maybe not. Every author I hear complaining about their situation looks like someone more interested in making excuses than they are in creating great work to me. The ones that don't complain are facing challenges just as difficult as the ones who are, but their focus is on what they can control instead of what they can't. Inevitably these are the ones that get more done and get better at their craft. While the haters languish in their own version of needing to be right, these are the folks who set aside their misconceptions in order to find their next highest truth.

This applies to every field of inquiry, of course. I just know I could spend hundreds of years getting better at writing books and never find an end to that improvement arc. So my interest in politics and science and medicine remains cursory, and I remain in a position that attempts to consider every point of view without clinging to any of them as absolute truths.

The last thing I want to do with the little bit of information I have been able to gather is form beliefs around them; that way, new information can enter my consciousness without challenging any long held beliefs. Rather than believe what anyone tells me, I reserve the right to consider both sides of an argument. Usually I end up realizing the two people arguing are each right in their own way, and also both wrong in their own way; which gives me more reason to reserve final judgement.

This works great for the fiction author, who will benefit a great deal from looking for thoughts that start with 'what if' instead of searching for ways to start our sentences with 'I know'. But it isn't just authors that reap the rewards of keeping an open mind; the world is full of creations that started out with a 'what if'. While the bulk of humanity focuses on being right about what is and isn't possible, the rare gem looks for ways to make what was considered impossible yesterday commonplace today.

As often as people level their criticisms against folks who are obsessed with inventing or improving products or services, they are typically spending at least twice that time depending on those inventions and improvements. One of the keys to getting more done in a day than most people is shrugging off the limitations others tend to adopt, and I suppose the most extreme examples tend to ignore more of those limits than anyone. When I think of how many things didn't exist when I was a kid that are completely commonplace now, my mind runs in place for a minute. Every one of those things were the product of an obsession and disbelief in some form, and they all just keep getting better due to imagination and hard work.

Goods and services aren't the only thing that benefit from streamlined thinkers. If you believe the story of almost any messiah, you have to consider how much intense inner work they must have each done to reach some significant level of enlightenment within one lifetime. Not only that, most of them get there in their twenties or thirties at the very latest; that's only a fraction of a lifetime, in modern terms. And their days were all only twenty-four hours, as well.

Many people believe their messiahs were born enlightened, of course; but that isn't how most of the stories actually go. Messiahs come to show us what we all can do and be, according to their own words; how rude would that attitude be if they were born with all those miraculous abilities? As often as Superman may be likened to a messiah, he never told the people of Earth all they had to do was try if they wanted to have his super powers. Every messiah does, though; which means they climbed a ladder we all can climb…or they're a bunch of tremendous assholes that want to watch us try.

If those stories are true, we all have it in us.

If they're not, they don't matter.

Either way, we each have twenty-four

hours in a day.

The real kicker in all this is that the people who work the hardest and make time management a high priority often have to start out making the least money. As much as the rest of us might depend on their brilliant products and innovations, the current system has no way to compensate idea people while they are having their ideas. Creatives have to do more than just have an idea; they have to find a way to implement it as well.

Even though their days are also only twenty-four hours long.

Nobody benefits from someone sitting around all day thinking of brilliant stuff but never doing anything to make it a reality. Whether you're a painter or a software designer or an author, being clever at your craft just isn't enough in the modern marketplace. You have to be clever at starting and running a business as well, as good at selling your product as you are at creating it. This is a reality the day jobber never has to grapple with; and when creative types finally get paid for all that time they put in, the working stiff often thinks they suddenly became the classic 'overnight success'.

Not every creative gets paid for the time they put in, and not every one should. A lack of good business sense or ethics or practices won't pay off no matter how long you keep at it; you have to get all your ducks in a row in a very real way to find any true success in your own business, and more fail than succeed. This is a gap that used to be bridged by a special relationship between a business owner and someone looking to learn the ropes of that business.

They used to be called apprentices, and still are in some fields; but these days we have taken to calling these folks interns. Instead of starting a business and failing, they step in to help someone run their existing company. They don't get paid much, or at all, when we look at the money side of things; but they gain invaluable knowledge and experience in their chosen field, and everything theoretically works out great for both the intern and the business owner.

Unless the government steps in, and puts the kibosh on the whole system. Then we've got another problem, which leads us to the next chapter.

#057: MINIMUM WAGE PREVENTS ENTRY INTO THE JOB MARKET!

In days of old, when knights were bold; and minimum wage was not invented. You worked for free, to learn a trade; and joblessness was prevented.

Yeah, I know that isn't how it goes; but that is sort of how it used to be. People had lots of kids to work the family farm or business, and those that wanted to pursue another life went off and sought out an apprenticeship.

Sometimes folks had to pay to learn from a professional, but a lot of times they were able to work at a reduced wage or no wage until they had developed a skill set of their own. At that point they could become an employee, and start to receive a decent wage; or they could open their own business and do more work for a bigger share.

The word 'apprentice' has a nice ring to it, but I guess certain fields didn't like the way it sounds as much as I do. Enter interns, who are in much the same boat as the apprentice without the cool name.

These folks worked in professional fields of all kinds for decades, starting with little or no skills and building themselves up into something marketable. Nobody raised any objections to the practice, which wasn't really new, until recently; hell, 'intern' was not even a commonly used word outside certain circles until one went down on a president.

But that's completely off topic, so let's leave it there.

Relationships like these can be very important when a singular legacy needs to be passed down, or a relatively unique skill needs to be taught by one of the few who know it.

More than once, I applied for a job I knew I could do well by offering to work free for a week. Every employer I offered that to told me it was not legal for them to do it, but the person considering me always told me they appreciated the offer.

I also got the job every time I did that, but I can't say whether or not that was the determining factor; I can say it didn't hurt.

People who see how much value they can offer by doing one thing often realize they can possibly offer more if they learn another. Rather than go into debt for schooling they don't really need, a lot of these people look for ways to learn that don't require them forking over a wad of cash or sacrificing their credit rating.

These people are apprentices and interns, clever people who realize they can learn a thing best by doing it; and they don't mind learning for little or no money. It's better than paying money out, after all.

Of course, there are potential problems in these situations. Where do we want to live, some cartoon world where the sun shines every day and everyone you meet is just like the last person you met?

There are potential problems in virtually every situation imaginable, but you can't throw this baby out with the bathwater.

Let the interns and apprentices that want to leave their situation be free to leave it, give the ones being harassed proper recourse; and let the rest keep working and learning.

It just makes sense, probably one of the reasons this practice has been around so long.

This is one of the few systems we don't need to meddle with that much. The relationship here is between teacher and student, and those are really the only individuals that should be concerned about who is getting paid what.

If anything, we should be encouraging this in other fields. Most of us know the father of modern medicine was a quack, but this was one of those few things he got right.

Doctors in Hippocrates' age were put through apprenticeships instead of courses, and learned their field in the field instead of in the classroom. We all might be in a better place if the practice had continued as he put it forth in that oath doctors don't take anymore.

Yet many people are making a fuss about these relationships, demanding that everyone working make at least minimum wage for their efforts. The truth is most folks don't have much to offer when they enter these programs, and paying them minimum wage is not practical for a business owner.

Meanwhile, no one is upset that business owners have no minimum wage; only that they aren't able to pay it to employees on every occasion.

Also, these folks aren't upset that demanding minimum wage for every worker slams shut many doors of opportunity that were open before. Young people have enough trouble making it in today's economy, and plenty of them are disillusioned with the whole setup they are supposed to inherit.

Taking away apprenticeships and internships is just telling these people they need to attend schools at a higher cost than any generation before, in an academic setting more removed from reality than ever.

It's no wonder many young adults don't see the point of pursuing the American dream; there almost isn't one, anymore. Even if they see the point, how are they supposed to see the path?

Previous generations have spent so much time making that path harder than ever to walk, building public school systems to create factory workers and collectively forgetting that rites of passage are important.

Pile that onto myths like 'if I can do it, so can you' while brushing aside important arguments like 'it takes a village' and 'the hero always gets lost', and it's no wonder young people are disillusioned with this illusory reality we all built together.

I suppose the next target is children, especially children of business owners. Once parents start being forced to pay their offspring minimum wage to do chores around the house or work in the store, we might just manage to ruin the next generation before they have come anywhere near adulthood.

I remember being a little shocked when I got my first job, since they paid by the hour instead of by the task. It didn't take long for me to start wondering why most of my coworkers were making as much or more than me, when many of them did so little actual work.

The pointlessness of it all hit me hard back then, but I finally saw a path to working harder and getting paid more for it once I'd been at it awhile.

Equality has been a pretty hot topic with Americans pretty much since the country was formed.

Ask nearly anyone, and they'll tell you they are all for equality. Put the word 'equality' by itself on a voting ballot, and everyone that votes will surely mark that box. Equality is a wonderful concept, no matter what pair of eyes you're looking out from.

Get a dozen people to explain equality, though…and you may have a bit of a problem on your hands. With a dozen different definitions, likely skewed in the direction of each person you asked, you might have a little trouble instituting practical policies or making meaningful laws that create actual equality.

The first thing we might need to do, when it comes to bringing about equality, is define it in terms we can all agree on. Discussing a subject that has as many definitions as there are people that know the word can be awkward, especially when the subject is an emotionally charged one.

And for anyone with an age or a sex or a skill that they associate themselves with, equality is most likely an emotionally charged issue. Nearly all of us have had instances of life not being fair in one way or another.

We'll talk more about that in the next chapter, how equality means something different to each of us and how it affects us all in different ways. There's one thing we can't really argue about, and it's the lesson I learned from getting paid by the hour for so many years. The truth is, no matter how we might decide to look at the subject…

#058: EQUALITY CREATES INEQUALITY!

That old quote we have all heard may be sexist, in that it excludes all those genders that aren't men; but even if we change 'all men are created equal' to 'all people are created equal', we still don't get any closer to the truth.

We each have unique DNA that gives us certain advantages and disadvantages right out of the gate, we each get raised in an environment that is not duplicated exactly even for siblings reared in the same household, and we all live in a world where what country you are born in says a lot about your options.

Does that sound like equality to you?

Alright, so we can dispense with that myth. What we can't push aside so easily is the concept of equality itself.

Most of us have some idea of what this

means to us, just as most of us feel some form of equality should be available to everyone. What we seem to get confused about is what kind of laws and rules should get instituted to enforce equality.

As harsh as it sounds, certain people and companies don't see equality like most of the rest of us do. They'll hire people based on race or gender or religious beliefs if someone doesn't stop them, or any other myriad of discriminating factors; and such practices can't be said to keep equality in mind at all.

What a lot of people don't understand is that we tend to group up by sex and race and religion, so we are kind of fighting some pretty basic instincts here; and it's hard to imagine someone wanting to work for an employer that doesn't want them around, but we've got to draw some lines somewhere.

Since we already have so many lines drawn by other people, I suppose we should start by learning to work within those established parameters.

We're already talking about jobs, so we should have a look at equality in the workplace. There are no laws enforcing equality of any kind among siblings, beyond fulfilling everyone's basic needs; but that's no surprise.

We already know children are more marginalized than anyone. They get their first real chance at some kind of equality in school, but none of that really matters much for most people.

Once we hit the workplace, we can start to see how things shake down in the real world.

Making sure everyone is being equally compensated for the work they do sounds both basic and fair. Anyone who has been part of a team knows it seldom is, however.

Most of us have discovered at some point that a coworker bent on doing nothing is somehow making more than us, or that the person who skips out early every day to pick up their kid from school is being paid as many hours as everyone else.

The first lesson most of us need to learn when we enter the workforce brings another old saying to mind, one that even a child should be familiar with.

Life isn't fair.

As much as that seems contrary to the concept of equality, we get mired in misperception if we continue to childishly insist that life be fair.

Watch a nature channel sometime; and just be grateful that when life isn't fair to us, the consequences are not nearly as dire as they are in that world. We might complain about those that feed on us figuratively, but we seldom have to worry about literally being eaten alive.

Some people can negotiate better than others, some people have a natural charisma that makes almost everyone like them; and finding any two people that learn a skill at exactly the same speed is like finding matching snowflakes in a blizzard.

Beyond that, we have to look at who puts the most care and attention to detail into a project. We have to consider who starts early and who stays late, and what each person does with the number of hours they do put in.

When we really start considering all the factors at play when it comes to getting even the simplest task completed, the only real way we can reach equality in the workplace is by issuing paychecks as unique as the individuals receiving them. Rather than say everyone should make the same amount, true equality in the workplace almost demands that no two people should be getting the same size paycheck.

If you pay lazy workers the same wage you pay the highest producers, you're rewarding the lazy for their laziness while punishing the producers for their productiveness. Clearly, this path leads to one collectively very lazy workforce if allowed to play out long term.

Then who's going to get the work done?

Of course, it's nice to think we all deserve a lot of love in our lives; but even this is a place where equal opportunity creates unequal outcomes.

Those of us who have spent time residing in a dark place or two know when we want love most we are least likely to find it, and that getting to a place where you can love yourself is an important first step on the path to loving someone else.

Nothing about any of that sounds fair, but it's the way of things nonetheless. Countless skills and practices come into play when you do find that someone, and those not up to the tasks are not able to keep it together.

Even those that are get blindsided every now and then, and good hearts break around the world every day.

What we really should be shooting for with all this equality talk is equal opportunity. Those that don't work to make opportunities come along or seize them when they do will see no reward in this kind of system, but objective reality demands that someone is producing those rewards that will get handed out somewhere along the line.

The only way to have those rewards is to create or produce some kind of results, so it only makes sense to reward the folks working hard to get results.

These people come from all walks of life, but no one can realistically deny that some of them started out with more opportunity than others. Many professional fields that require extensive schooling are flooded with folks with parents willing and able to pay that high price, and the increasing cost of college makes this situation a little worse for everyone with each passing year.

Others get grants or loans or scholarships, but even these opportunities are not available to everyone. As much as I might dislike the current educational system, I am still fully aware that many professions specifically require such an investment just to get to that first day on the job.

Privileged kids may often grow up to be privileged adults, and the upper class in this country is pretty typically made up of people who were raised in upper class households. However, there is an anomaly that happens a little too often to be called an anomaly.

What about all those people who start with nothing and become ultra rich? The story has been told so many times it's almost a cliche, but somehow most of us never tire of hearing some new version of it.

The real mind bender here is that these are the most classic examples of equal opportunity, and what can be accomplished through obsessive hard work no matter where you come from.

But before we can celebrate that, we have to look at how most of these stories start out. Some of us may envy these people their success; but no one envies them the harsh conditions they often began in.

Nearly every great success has an origin story peppered with trauma of some kind, almost to the point where the fan of these stories and people have to wonder if early tragedy is an essential component to later success.

We can't go back and engineer our own early tragedy, and it would be pretty crazy of us to want to; but we can make life easier for ourselves if we're willing to make life hard first. Of course, that's a subject for another chapter. I hope you have a few more minutes, so you can read it now.

#060: MAKING LIFE HARD MAKES LIFE EASIER!

Two opposing desires exist in each of us, to some degree; the desire to rise to a challenge, and the desire to do as little as possible. Some people know what it feels like to work every day from the time they wake up until the day is through, sleeping as few hours as they can so they can hit it hard again first thing in the morning. Others are familiar with the habit of doing next to nothing, spending all day avoiding challenges most folks don't even consider all that challenging.

Then there's the rest of us, stuck somewhere in the middle trying to figure out a way to strike a balance of some sort between doing too much and doing nothing at all. We know there is a time for work and a time for relaxing, but we also believe that one exists to complement the other. Laying around all day only feels like a reward if we have earned it with hard work, and working hard all day only feels worth it if we get a little chill time afterwards.

If you're anything like me, you might really admire the people who use their days to get a lot done. You might even be grateful when accomplished people write books about how they got where they are, and describe the methods they used to lift themselves from the place they were to the place they wanted to be. Most of those books have a lot of commonalities, especially when the person writing them was trying to become successful in more than one aspect of their life. You could even sum up the overall common thread of these stories with a single sentence, like I did to title this post.

Making life hard makes life easier!

That hardly sounds like good news to the common couch potato, but the rest of us can extrapolate some valuable tips on living better from this simple statement. Most of us know life is safer and easier now than it has been in any other period of recorded history. We may not have all the same opportunities as those that came before us, but we enjoy the benefits of their social progress and technological discoveries like they never could. We take advantages they never dreamed of for granted, and most of us will never know what it's like to ride a wagon train across the country or wait weeks to hear news about an ailing relative whose doctor is treating them with leeches.

Of course, the argument exists that those folks didn't have time to binge watch their favorite shows or check multiple social media accounts several times a day. Almost everything took more effort yesterday than it does today, and there isn't really all that much history between the lifestyle that had to grow and kill its own food to the modern person that can get a week's worth of groceries in twenty minutes at the supermarket.

And don't tell me you're vegan, and aren't some kind of murderer; just because you can't hear lettuce scream doesn't mean you aren't eating life to live exactly like everyone else. Besides, the fact that so many people can be so choosy about what they eat is simply another testament to how easy life is in the modern day. You can look to other parts of the world and point out how many people are starving there, but here in America poverty and obesity go together like peanut butter and jelly. We can thank those that came before us for all of this, but we also have to consider what we will pass down that future generations can thank us for.

Now we live with all these modern conveniences, and we have to find some way to fill all that time we have been given by those that came before us. Staring at screens of various sizes can eat up most or all that time if we want it to, but we might be missing the point of all the exhaustive effort that went into creating this easy life for us. For the first time in maybe ever, we have a chance to take care of all the essentials and still have plenty of hours left in a day. As appealing as it is to spend a bunch of time telling others how they should behave, we might do well to spend those hours on ourselves instead.

That's my polite way of saying that being a social justice warrior often comes at the price of stunted personal evolution, and that the only real perfection is something we can only strive for in our own behavior.

We all know working out on Wednesday makes us feel better on Thursday, that eating real food today will benefit us tomorrow, and that sitting quietly every day can drastically cut down on mental drama. Very few people don't have some idea of what they could do to improve themselves, but the knowledge stands in direct opposition to the desire to do as little as possible to get what we need to do done. Although we each have our own standards for how much we should get done in a day, we also all have a point where it's just too much. Striking a balance might be as important as pushing that line a little further in the direction we want to grow, since overdoing it can have drastic consequences as well.

One of my favorite things to do is wake up early and write. It isn't a favorite activity because I don't enjoy sleeping in, or because I like to place rigorous demands on my brain before anyone expects me to even be awake. In fact, I love sleeping in almost as much as I love lazy mornings. But sleeping in and having a lazy morning only feels good when it is a reward for a series of mornings where I got up and got stuff done.

Each of us has an idea of how we should be living, whether we are an inspiration to others or an example of what not to do. The funny thing is, we all have different ideas around both accomplishment and relaxation. It may be true that everyone knows the path while few actually walk it, but it's also pretty clear that the ideal path for each of us is uniquely our own. Blend all these distinctly different ideas with a widely varying motivation to both get things done and make life easier, and you get a pretty confusing bowl of thought soup.

But, hey…

Who ever said life is supposed to be easy to understand?

#062: THE WORLD IS ALWAYS ENDING!

Human beings have seen some pretty scary stuff through the ages. Even if climate change made it possible for us to exist in the first place, subsequent shifts haven't always treated us kindly. We have yet to see what will happen next, of course; but odds show us it's probably one of two possibilities. They aren't the only two possibilities; but they are the two most likely ways this will all play out.

The first is that today's doom predictors will be wrong. Most of them have been in the past, to everyone's relief; but at some point some of them will be right, and that's bad news for all of us. Science is actually based largely on theories, and those are pretty shaky foundations; but when you add political or financial pressure to the mix, scientists will say pretty much anything you want them to. Not to say there's anything wrong with that; if you threatened my family or livelihood or offered me enough money, I'd probably tell people whatever you wanted me to as well. Scientists are no more or less human than the rest of us.

Also, sometimes they're just wrong.

Or they find a solution. It can be hard to tell when the first scenario happens or when the second one does, but recent generations can all attest to having borne the weight of one situation or the other. Nuclear war got staved off, and the ozone layer seems to be holding out; but people today are talking about climate change with as much fervor as people of yesterday talked about those issues, and even they haven't been properly resolved yet.

Surely a few folks are certain an asteroid will hit before any of that happens, but plenty of people worry about nuclear war given the current political climate. Never mind that those words could have applied to any moment in history since the atomic bomb was invented; there's stuff going on now, and it could mean the end!

The question here isn't whether or not

the world will end. Let me save you the suspense: the world will definitely end. People will be long gone by then, either snuffed out by circumstance or because we finally found a way to go interstellar; but we won't want to be here at that point, when the sun turns into a black hole and consumes what used to be our planet. And who knows; any variety of things could happen sooner that would obliterate what we call the Earth.

However, it probably won't be us.

When we say there are enough nuclear weapons to destroy the world many times over, we're really kind of stretching things. We might destroy all living things, but we won't vaporize the planet itself. After another climate shift or two, life might just start all over with no memory of what came before. There may even be enough future ahead of our planet for it all to happen several more times before the Earth actually breaks up into little pieces or gets eaten by the sun. It might even have happened several times before, as far as we know.

But that isn't the question here.

I want to know why so many people are and apparently always have been obsessed with the end of the world. I'll give you that it's a thought that hurts to think about, and admit to a peculiar fascination with all the subjects that fall under that big umbrella; but what's the point of obsessing over this one in particular? What's the best case scenario? Are people hoping for the day when their skin melts off their face for whatever reason, so they can finally run down the streets screaming about how they told us this would happen?

There's nothing good about being right in this scenario, and the only people who should be obsessed with it are the people willing to dedicate their lives to doing something about it. Turning potential global catastrophe into a political issue is no way for either side to solve it, and it leaves the rest of us somewhere in the middle wondering if most people just love a good fight. Conspiracy theorists will tell you that the people in control are just trying to make sure everyone is constantly afraid, and the temptation to believe them might come from a good place. After all, otherwise a bunch of people have done this to themselves.

For every scientist willing to admit they don't really know what's going on, there are countless uninformed people eager to explain their version of how things are going to play out. Never mind that they would have been singing some other tune if they had been born a generation earlier, and an even different one if they had come a generation before that; there's a chance they could be right, which means one thing and one thing only.

You don't have much time in their doom and gloom scenario, so you should use it wisely. Imagine all the hours one human being has spent listening to another human being talk about the end of the world since the world has started ending, without it ever actually coming to pass; then try to estimate how many lifetimes that adds up to, and let your mind boggle a bit. Then briefly consider this next possibility, as you walk away from the pointless encounter.

Perhaps we're not the pinnacle of creation. We can consider that the climate changed to accommodate us, so why can't we project the possibility that it's changing again to get ready for the next thing? Those big lizards were not something we could have competed with effectively; and even if we could have, it would have meant wiping them out or keeping a few in preserves. You just can't have skyscrapers and dinosaurs in the same world, no matter how much of a humanitarian you consider yourself. We have to entertain the idea that we are the dinosaurs in the next scenario. Maybe our bumbling ways would smash the sensitive little folks coming after us, in so many ways; or maybe they'd be forced to smash us.

Or maybe robots just like it hot.

Either way, talking about the end of the world should really be reserved for the very few people willing and able to do something to prevent it. And they should talk about it amongst themselves, in private; that way we can suspect there are quiet heroes out there coming up with solutions for every situation and making sure each generation survives its unique threat. As long as the world continues to exist, we can all relax knowing they are on the job. Like a nerdy Avengers…but again, with less bragging.

Part of the reason so many people live in a state of fear is because staying informed about this kind of thing is next to impossible. We have minds designed to know stuff, and it's hard to admit we don't have all the facts when we already have an opinion. Many of us rely on other people to curate our information for us, even if most of us know the people doing the curating almost always have some stake in the game themselves.

Out of all the people willing to comment on virtually every subject, very few are experts in any of them. Often the only ones willing to admit they don't know are the experts; but they're happy to take several hundred pages to say so, if the money is right. And whoever curates our information can extract whatever they want from that study, and even quote directly from its pages; while the other side can cite the same study and draw completely different conclusions.

Most importantly, though…everyone gets paid.

Maybe making everything so complicated is a good way to get things done, and maybe not. The world hasn't ended, despite the conviction of many people throughout history; so there is that. Yet I have to wonder what the benefit of all this information is if no one is really doing much of anything with it.

Government studies no one actually reads are one thing, but the bills and laws they write are quite another. They can also stretch to hundreds of pages, and many of these things are put to a public vote. Politicians may be embarrassed to admit they didn't read the whole thing, but voters seldom are. Although they feel comfortable weighing in, they just don't have the kind of time it would take to read what they're voting on.

I would say you should take a moment to let that sink in, but I'm sure you already have long since done so. These aren't secrets, after all; they're thoughts that hurt to think. We all know the world can be a messed up place, and that we are expected to live with certain knowledge that doesn't make much sense. So we'll talk about voting in this country next, in a chapter called…

#063: VOTERS DON'T READ WHAT THEY VOTE ON!

Quite a few people think voting is important, whether the system those votes are being cast in is perfect or floundering or completely corrupt. They think weighing in has an impact, and they often feel those who don't vote are in no position to complain or wish things were different.

Granted, this is a good point...shades of grey not withstanding. A lot of people in the world don't have the right to vote on much of anything, and some folks believe that opportunity should not be taken for granted in any circumstance.

Other people think participating in a corrupt or broken power structure is giving credit where it isn't due, and that voting empowers a system we should be focused on disempowering.

They are waiting for good options, instead of resorting to choosing between the lesser of two evils. Or maybe they really just don't care. Many of us know 49% of Americans don't vote, and maybe this is one of the reasons why; but those folks aren't really part of this discussion.

Then there is everyone in between, who may have their political viewpoints but aren't so adamant about others needing to think the way they do. These folks probably make up the majority of voters in America, and they take a few minutes from their otherwise busy lives to weigh in on matters of great importance when the booths open up.

Of all these people, and all the issues being voted on, you might start to wonder just how many of the voters understand what they are weighing in on. While they might get a summary of what a bill says or a glimpse of how a politician acts in public, it's kind of hard to believe that anyone who votes is forming their opinion based on all the facts on hand.

With those previously mentioned busy lives most of us have going on, very few people can really say they have a good grasp on politics.

Even the politicians often admit they spend most of their time raising money, whether to run their campaign or prepare for the next one or fund their office or line their own pockets. Once they get in there, they have to fight to stay in there; many of our elected officials can't be bothered with reading every page of every bill or law they vote on.

Maybe an aide reads the whole thing, but that doesn't give the official a deep understanding of what direction society will be guided in by this action; more likely the vote will be swayed by the influence of someone they owe a favor to, or who they want to call on later.

Speaking of bills and laws, have you ever tried to read one in its entirety? The issue was highlighted when a recent tax bill got voted on, because the people voting didn't have time to read it; but who realistically has time to read that sort of thing?

And how long can you focus when you're reading a document that drones on for hundreds of pages? Any writer knows you've got to keep things interesting for at least a few people, but that is a ridiculously small demographic.

I have yet to meet anyone who has read every word of every item they ever voted on, and I'm not sure I want to meet that rare person anyways.

It's almost as though someone is deliberately making things too confusing to keep proper track of. Maybe I'm ridiculously naive, but shouldn't people understand what they're voting on?

Also, shouldn't we weigh in on these things one at a time? Many people vote on something not because of the main issue but because something has been tacked onto it that affects them directly.

Others change their minds after finding out the thing they wanted to see pass means increased taxes for their particular group, or carries some other unfavorable consequence. Although we all want to see this nation get better, few of us want to be singled out as having to pay for all the improvements.

Rather than let proposed laws and bills run on for literally hundreds of pages, we might make a law that all proposals must be concise and make sense. We might even make a rule that they should each be separate items on the ballot, although that itself should be a separate item on the ballot.

Voting on a hundred little issues instead of a few big ones may sound like a bit of a pain, and it might require a little more engaged reading; but it would at least create a scenario where people have an opportunity to understand what they're voting on without needing someone to sum it up for them.

As complicated as getting three hundred fifty million people on the same page about anything may be, this system complicates things even more. If you did find a person who had made the time to read every article put to a vote, you can bet they could not have possibly had time to read all the existing laws on record in America.

When I first heard what we'll be talking about next, I was a little dumbfounded. As the years passed, I had my own little moments of terror as I did some thing or another that may have been illegal. I knew the only people who understood all the laws in any given area were lawyers, and even they had to choose a specialty if they hoped to really get a grasp on some aspect of the legal system in this country.

Then I realized it's just another thought that hurts to think, and I found some ways to laugh about it.

#065: AMERICA HAS MORE LAWS THAN ANY COUNTRY IN HISTORY!

As tempting as it is to echo the sentiments of generations past when we talk about the United States, the truth is the country changes so much so quickly that we need to drop all those old sayings to really sum up what America is all about today. This nation may have been founded on certain principles, and may have even held tight to those principles for some time; but power corrupts, and the dual temptation of power and profit turned out to be impossible to resist in this case. Even if it changed the entire thrust of what America was once all about, succumbing to these temptations was simply too appealing for our politicians as a whole.

America was once the land of the free. People living here at the time were so proud of that distinction they adopted the phrase, and passed it down. Hell, it's even in our theme song. Now people still say it, even if folks in other countries boast more freedoms than us while our government institutes laws that removes more of our liberties with each passing year. This seems to be another case of perception being at odds with reality, and we know how hard it is to change beliefs once we let them firm up. Even if we have to admit that our national anthem is starting to sound like propaganda when you hold it up next to the behavior of today's government, we also need to look at the truth behind the myth.

Can we call it the land of the free, if we have more written restrictions against citizen behavior than any other country ever? Can freedom really be enforced with more laws? If so, maybe we are on the right track. Nearly everyone knows we have more laws on record than any other country in history, but somehow this is not the main topic of discussion when we talk about how we can make this country better. Instead more rules get suggested, and often make it into the books. Rather than supplant old laws that don't make sense anymore, they just get added to the pile.

Any good social historian will tell you that every government has to make a choice, and stand for something. The first issue at hand when it comes to establishing who you are as a territory is whether you want to collectively choose freedom or security. Freedom is good, of course; people should be allowed to do as they please, right?

Well, yes and no.

Most of us agree we should end that phrase with 'as long as it doesn't hurt anyone else' or something like that. Yet as soon as we qualify the phrase, we contradict it. That's really just another way to say you want both freedom and security, in a world where you just can't have both.

Alright, so we need to find some sort of balance. If total freedom is complete chaos, and total security is absolute control…how do we find some place in the middle we can all agree on?

Well, we can't. Not really. We've all heard of the old laws that do get removed from the books. They sound super silly to us, in the modern age. Yet even if they have been removed from most books, they remain in others. How many times have you heard of a state law decreeing that a man and woman are considered married after they have spent one night together? Or a city law forbidding spitting in the street? Or a state law preventing people from being drunk in public?

Many of those laws have been rolled back in a lot of places, but all of the above still exist somewhere in these United States. Meanwhile new ones are springing up all the time, and they don't exactly have the same spirit behind them that the old laws did. The people who started this country really just wanted folks to be decent to each other, as far as we can tell by reading their laws. A woman's sexual reputation was a different thing in those times, we all know it's only polite to act sober when you're drunk in public, and very few people think spitting in the street isn't gross.

What happens is that society moves forward in certain ways, and the rules have to be changed along with those movements. Before the stock market existed, insider trading wasn't something we needed laws against; when it was mostly men in the workplace, sexual harassment was not really an issue. As reality morphs, laws have to be created to define its new boundaries; that is perfectly understandable. But the laws a society makes says a lot about the overall character of that society, and the number of rules a nation puts in the books must say something about the people writing the laws.

Whether this implies we are the most enlightened nation ever or the one most apt to flounder in its own excessive wordiness, I don't know for sure. The fact remains that we have more laws on the books than any county in history, which puts the average citizen in a similar boat to the one they row down to the voting booth. Just as we can't be surprised that voters don't read what they vote on, we also can't be too shocked to find out some people are criminals without even knowing it. With so many laws on the books, even a legal expert can't keep track of all of them. How is the common person who just wants to be a good law abiding citizen supposed to find time to memorize all those laws, in between work and family and reading the articles they vote on?

I always love to offer a solution, especially when it happens to strike me as both funny and ridiculously impractical. In the spirit of such fun, let me put forth an idea to help everyone with this.

You know how some traffic laws differ from state to state, and there will sometimes be a series of signs telling you what those differences are just as you cross over into another state? How about we make every state put all their laws on signs, and line them up along the side of each freeway or highway that takes travelers across the border? That way they have to make them concise, and short enough to put on a road sign; also, it might cause the people making the laws to think twice about the rules they are making for other people to live by.

There's only so much space on the side of the road, after all.

Since we're getting near the end here, I think lightening things up again might be a good idea. The last thing I want to do is leave you thinking I am obsessed with politics, or that I have even a passing interest in the subject.

Instead, let's talk about the weather.

#067: WEATHER FORECASTERS GET PAID TO BE WRONG!

The last thing anyone can expect from anyone else is complete consistency. We are human, after all; and mistakes are part of that reality. Most of us learn from those mistakes, and do our best to make sure we don't make them again. We apologize to the people affected by our missteps, and do our best to make up for whatever damage we did by overestimating our own abilities or letting something slip our minds.

Except weather forecasters, of course.

No other profession is built on a history of being wrong and still getting to come to work the next day. We already know most people take the fact that politicians are liars for granted in this country, but now we need to look at the difference between outright lying and just being wrong about the thing you say you're an expert in. Political candidates can make erroneous predictions as well: like squashing a more popular candidate's campaign because they are sure they have it locked down, or not treating an opponent with the respect they deserve because they're confident they have it in the bag; but politicians pay the ultimate price for such arrogance, and they end up not getting the job at all.

Weather forecasters are a whole different deal, though. They may have gotten more attractive overall as the years have passed, but that isn't really the improvement most of us were hoping for. As nice as it may be to have hot women give us our news, it would be even nicer if they were better at it than their male counterparts. That just isn't the case, however; instead we get new faces telling us the same old lies, and the fact that they are pretty doesn't take away from the fact that they're also often wrong. I may be alone in this, but I wouldn't mind unattractive people giving me accurate weather predictions. If the content itself doesn't matter, I may as well watch news in a language I can't understand; the way the women dress on those stations makes it pretty clear most people aren't watching because of their interest in current events.

Many of us remember the big deal many news stations made about a certain radar system back when it was new. All the larger stations tried to be early adopters, hoping to leave their competition in the dust as they wielded this unique new technology; but no matter how fancy their lingo or images got, they still relied heavily on their reputation for being wrong. Now every station seems to have it, and somehow inaccurate predictions remain just as popular. It's a good thing comedy headed a whole different direction; if they had followed the way of the weather forecaster, we would have a bunch of prop comics who weren't funny dominating the scene instead of the hilarious folks we are so lucky to have.

Over the years, I have lived in a few different places. Some of them have been pretty predictable, as far as weather goes. Yet…even when I lived in Seattle, the weather forecasters were known for getting it wrong. I mean, all they have to say is that it will be overcast with a damn good chance of rain in that area; they would be right over seventy percent of the time. Instead they try to get all specific, and shoot themselves in the foot as much as other areas as they erroneously predict temperatures and storm schedules. Why not just tell folks to dress in layers and carry an umbrella, since they know the city will generally be cold and wet?

I thought all this would change when I moved to California. Once again, weather forecasters in most parts of the state should have it pretty easy: in late April or early May, they could just record themselves saying it should be nice and sunny all week in dozens of different outfits. While they sat on a beach and sipped margaritas, the news station could play a different version of the recording each week. Instead they say it will be ninety-five degrees and it actually hits a hundred, predict summer storms that never happen and fail to predict the ones that do. I mean…why be specific when you're just going to end up being wrong?

Sometimes they're right on, of course; but even a broken clock is right twice a day, as they say. That hasn't led to a trend of people hanging broken clocks on their walls, so they can get the time right every once in a while. Nonetheless, weather forecasters are more secure in their jobs than ever before; as we watch the news lean increasingly towards opinion instead of facts, these predictably inaccurate prognosticators seem to fit in better than ever. Instead of being the awkward and out of place step-sibling, the rise in fake news has made these folks the most respectable member of the family.

After all, we expect them to be wrong.

Most of us have driven by a business with one of those signs in the window that says 'Psychic' in glowing neon letters. Very few of us have actually stopped in and paid money to get our palms or tea leaves read, but obviously someone is: every city has psychics, just like every city has weather people; and the signs keep burning in the window year after year. I can't help but wonder how one brand of prognosticator became a pillar of the community while the other gets sniggered at by a bunch of otherwise decent people who watch the news. It would be no more strange to me to have a psychic show up on a broadcast laden in robes and chicken bones than it is to have the weather predictors step on the stage with their snazzy outfits and green screens. They could make all kinds of projections for tomorrow, be right every once in a while, and just keep on coming to work every day.

Exactly like weather forecasters.

I have worked various jobs in my lifetime, and each time I got more skilled or specialized it meant I had to be right about more things more often. No matter what field we're talking about, the best practitioners almost always bear the burden of having to be consistently correct. When they're wrong, they have to own up to it and make whatever effort is required to make it right. Any professional in virtually any field has to know what they're doing and what they're talking about, or their reputation will suffer for it; except weather forecasters, of course.

Please don't suggest that psychics are respected professionals, either. Even I have to admit that if I met a local weather personality and a psychic at the same party, I would rather talk to the former. They might be just as full of it as the latter, but it's okay to be seen in public with the weather person. The last thing any of us want is people whispering that we believe in people who claim they can predict the future, after all.

All I want is the occasional apology, really. The most annoying thing about weather people is that they show up for work the next day acting just as confident as they did the day before, despite the fact that yesterday they said it would be sunny today and now it's raining. If they would just start out their segment of the broadcast with a shrug and a brief, "hey, sorry about what I said yesterday", I might come away from the experience with a little more sympathy for forecasters.

I warned you the end was nearing, and we're getting pretty close to wrapping up this volume. Before we begin the end, I'd like to say a few words by way of introduction.

Saving the best for last is not really my thing, since I think each of these chapters address something important in its own way; that being said, I have been looking forward to sharing the title post with you since this whole concept got started.

The next chapter didn't originate as a blog post, like nearly all the others. It was actually going to influence the way I titled the entire series of books, and how I branded the blog.

Fortunately...I came to my senses, and changed my mind.

Making up a word is seldom a great way to get people to remember it, unless it has a particular ring to it. Also, marketing and advertising are hard enough without getting an email from every platform saying you have a misspelling in your title.

When I came up with 'Thoughts That Hurt To Think', I knew I had solved this problem. You may be able to find some of them still up on my website, depending on when you read this; but you can definitely find them in other books by me ending in '...and other thoughts that hurt to think'.

Now let's go back to the very beginning of all this, and talk about where words come from.

#074: WORDS ARE MADE UP!

It must have been a delightful moment when the first word was uttered. I wonder what it was? Fire? Food? Water? You know what's really funny? The first time the first word was spoken, it wasn't a word at all. It was just a sound, probably akin to a grunt, and probably made while someone was pointing at someone or something. It didn't become a word until someone else understood what the grunter meant by that sound, and agreed upon that meaning. Then they could use the same sound to mean the same thing, and they both got it.

Time to spread the word!

But how? You can't tell people about your new word; there aren't words to explain, or describe. Your word is the first one, and you've got a whole concept to get across before you can start using it regularly.

What are words, anyway? Well, they're agreements. They communicate our ideas without us having to be telepathic, or draw pictures for each other all day. But words are so much more than that, and every single one of them has a history all its own. They all have translations, or almost all of them, in thousands of different languages around the world. Can you imagine? Every single word had to be thought up, sounded out, agreed upon and then used commonly enough to not fall out of practice. Each word had to evolve, in each language, in its own way. Why? Because reading and writing came way after speaking, and there was no way to jot it down!

Back before there were words, there were campfires. They weren't really campfires, though; since those folks weren't really camping. They were living in some of the harshest conditions imaginable, with no worries about the sun burning out or alien invasion. They didn't have the time or the technology to be on social media, but they did have some opportunities we don't have today.

Like making up words. Those

campfires that weren't really campfires were probably the birth place of so many of our spoken and written friends, as folks gathered around after a hard day hunting and gathering. They had experiences and feelings to share, and no way to get it all off their chests without some serious grunting and flailing about. Since all the folks in the village needed to use the fire for warmth and to heat food, it was a natural gathering place.

It was also the first captive audience.

You can be sure as soon as words got invented, some imaginative tribe member started telling stories. Maybe they were true, and maybe they weren't; most likely they were a little of both, as are most stories. It must have been wonderful the first time someone sat down, told a story and made everyone forget themselves for a moment as they listened. They must have all sensed the magic of the situation, the special first that was happening around their guttering little campfire.

Or maybe the story was terrible, had a bunch of plot holes and went nowhere. That's probably more likely, with the scant availability of words back them. It must have really slowed down the telling of even the best story, having to stop and explain the new words you had to make up to get the tale across properly. Things didn't really get going for the campfire storyteller until much later.

Then came writing, and reading, and a whole new way to tell stories. Now here we are in the age of ebooks, and what's finally coming back around?

That's right, audio! More and more folks are getting into audiobooks now, and getting back in touch with their roots. Maybe they're even starting campfires in their backyards and listening to their favorite books.

Probably not, though.

Even so, I'd like to point out that things have finally come back around. I've always thought of myself as a modern day campfire storyteller, gifted with long glimpses into other worlds that I get to share with folks who love the same kinds of stories I do. In that spirit, I'd like to point out that there are still some words out there just waiting to be formed.

Like 'obviousity'. It's something that's obvious, only in object noun form. It's like turning 'need' into 'necessity', or like transforming 'absurd' into 'absurdity'.

Yeah, it's definitely more like that.

Just because the dictionary doesn't acknowledge it doesn't mean it doesn't make sense as a word. I can even use it effectively in a sentence, or a book title: 'Earth is in Space…and Other Mind-Blowing Obviousities'.

That was the original title I came up with for the first book in this series, and I liked it a lot. Then I put together the blog series title, and realized I liked 'Earth is in Space! And Other Thoughts That Hurt To Think' even better. It gave me the chance to tie all these together with the second half of the title, and link them to the blog as well. I know that isn't usually the way things are done; generally you would put the common part first, and the unique part as the subtitle; but you can still tell the books go together.

It's an obviousity.

Of course, I have been using the word a lot since coming up with it. The way it was created and the way I continue to use it still stand, even if it's not part of a book title. I reached for the word that would say what I wanted it to, and it wasn't there. Like countless people throughout history have. And as countless people throughout history have also done, I discovered that the word I needed did not exist.

So I made it up.

Like countless people throughout history have done.

Now you know what it means, if that in itself was not an obviousity; and hopefully you agree. Once that is established, you and I have taken steps together to make a new word.

That's how words are made, after all.

Dear Reader,

Every book says something about the person who wrote it. Some authors don't like to admit that, but they're generally the ones who reveal themselves the most. Others know it's an occupational hazard, and accept it along with all the other wonderful things that come with sharing a part of yourself through writing.

Then there are people like me.

I don't just want to weave my wonderings into fiction works, and my experiences into stories packed with powerful life lessons; I also want to share the difficult and awkward stuff. Fantasy can be a great escape, and inspiration certainly has its place; but all those other things need to be in the mix, too.

My favorite part of reading is coming upon some passage about something that I thought only I had ever thought about. Even when you don't particularly love the author that wrote it, it can be nice to know someone else out there has considered some problem or possibility you have contemplated before. It's why I love comedy, almost as much as I love books; both comedians and authors are allowed to push the envelope, and even expected to at times.

I don't consider myself a comedian, but I do so love to laugh. At the same time, I also can't help but think about the kind of subject matter in the pages you just finished reading. This book represents a unique opportunity to me, to share in a way I otherwise couldn't.

Now that you have read it, a special circle has closed for me. I would like to thank you for that, and leave you knowing I'm hoping we meet again soon.

Thanks for reading!

All the best,
Jay

Also available from Jay Norry...

Stumbling Backasswards Into the Light

Earth is in Space!
(and other thoughts that hurt to think)

As J.K. Norry

Dreaming the Perpetual Dream

The Ringer series
Ringing in a Voyage
Ringing in a New Year

Zombie Zero
Zombie Zero: The First Zombie
Zombie Zero: The Last Zombie
Zombie Zero: The Short Stories, Volumes 1-6

The Walking Between Worlds trilogy
Demons & Angels (Book I)
Rise of the Walker King (Book II)
Fall of the Walker King (Book III)

Learn more about Jay at **www.JayNorry.com**
Sign up to get exclusive content, the weekly newsletter, and much more
http://eepurl.com/T3NdD

www.ingramcontent.com/pod-product-compliance
Lightning Source LLC
Chambersburg PA
CBHW021152080526
44588CB00008B/302